CW01677009

TRIUMPH
Herald and Vitesse

TRIUMPH
Herald and Vitesse

Herald, 1200, 12/50, 13/60;
Vitesse, 2-litre

Graham Robson

OSPREY

Published in 1985 by Osprey Publishing Limited
12–14 Long Acre, London WC2E 9LP
Member company of the George Philip Group

Sole distributors for the USA

Motorbooks International
Publishers & Wholesalers Inc
Osceola, Wisconsin 54020, USA

© Copyright Graham Robson 1985

This book is copyrighted under the Berne Convention. All rights reserved. Apart from any fair dealing for the purpose of private study, research, criticism or review, as permitted under the Copyright Act, 1956, no part of this publication may be reproduced, stored in a retrieval system, or transmitted in any form or by any means, electronic, electrical, chemical, mechanical, optical, photocopying, recording or otherwise without prior written permission. All enquiries should be addressed to the publisher.

British Library Cataloguing in Publication Data
Robson, Graham
Triumph Herald and Vitesse.—(Osprey classic library)
1. Triumph Herald automobile—History
2. Triumph Vitesse automobile—History
I. Title
629.2′222 TL215.T7
ISBN 0-85045-636-3

Editor Tim Parker
Design Stonecastle Graphics

Filmset by
Tameside Filmsetting Ltd, Ashton-under-Lyne, Lancashire
Printed by
BAS Printers Ltd, Over Wallop, Hampshire

Contents

Introduction

In a way, I suppose, I owe my involvement in motoring journalism to the Triumph Herald, so it was almost inevitable that I would salute it, in book form, one day.

I went to work at Standard-Triumph in May 1961, as a development engineer, immediately after the Herald 1200 had been launched, and at once became involved in the evolution of the Vitesse, the Spitfire, and the rest of the family. From there I moved into the competitions department, and after that—writing!

There was a time when it was fashionable to sneer at the Herald, and there was also a time when it was ignored completely. Now, a full generation after it was first launched, its reputation has been revived, and its true worth is becoming clear. Amid the drama of corporate upheavals at Standard-Triumph between 1960 and 1962, the Herald was at once a villain and a hero. It was the villain because its launch had necessitated massive expansion, and the use of untried body-building methods, but it was eventually the hero when it, and its derivatives, provided the base for a whole new generation of Triumphs to come along later in the 1960s.

I salute the Herald as a remarkable concept, and an altogether remarkable car. At a time when Standard-Triumph needed an eye-catching new car, yet could find no-one to build the bodyshell for them, the Herald's concept—separate chassis, and a bodyshell built from several major sub-assemblies—was a flash of genius, and a really brave effort.

Not only that, but it was a great success. Certainly the first 948 cc cars had quality deficiencies, and even the devotees now agree that they were under-powered, but all the other cars had a great deal of charm, character, and real merit.

There is, of course, the controversial question of the handling. Towards the end of its life, it was usual for motoring writers to talk about the 'dangerous' Herald handling—but I doubt if any of the long-serving members of my fraternity ever looked back to what they had said in the early days of the project.

The fact is that when the Herald was conceived and launched, the idea of independent rear suspension, by swing axles, was a real advance compared with conventional British engineering of the day. It was only later in the 1960s, when the nimbleness of cars like the Mini, and the sophistication of Superminis all round Europe, had changed standards completely, that the criticism started up in earnest.

In all other respects, in any case, the Herald and Vitesse family was outstandingly successful. The cars had crisp Italian styling, at a time when other manufacturers were still British, and bulbous. They sold well, and continued to sell well, for over a decade. By any standards, they must have raked in millions of pounds of profit for their sponsors.

Now, in the 1980s, they are ideal machines for the 'classic car' fraternity to cherish. Compared with cars like the Morris Minor, the VW Beetle, and the Mini, their separate chassis construction gives them more potential durability. Compared with almost any other British car, they offer a wider choice of body styles, or engine specifications.

Acknowledgements

At my age, I really must try not to be so naïve.

When I started preparing this book, I thought it would be relatively straightforward—it is, after all, the sixth Triumph title I have produced—but I found that I still needed a lot of help to bring all the facts together. Now I would like to thank many people for all that assistance.

The book, of course, has been 25 years in the making, for I have always had connections with the Herald family of cars. In my time at the Triumph factory, not only did I run all the derivatives, and help to develop some of them, but I talked to many of the personalities of the day.

The most important, of course, were Alick Dick (who was 'ex' managing director by the time I first met him), Harry Webster, and John Lloyd, though John Carpenter, Lyndon Mills and Ray Henderson have all helped too.

Many of the photographs in these pages are from the Triumph archive. My good friend Norman James died before I started, again, to trawl through his records, but nonetheless I would like to thank Cyril Comley, Harry Mills, and their colleagues for their help during 1985.

John Weait and Angela Wigley helped smooth the path of research inside the company, while Anders Clausager of the British Motor Industry Heritage Trust helped me to locate certain archives, and statistical information. It also goes without saying that this book would have been more hearsay than correct reporting if I could not have researched the Standard-Triumph directors' minute books, held at the University of Warwick's Modern Records Department, supervised by Richard Storey and Alistair Tough.

John Griffiths, president of the Triumph Sports Six Club, his fellow members Bill Sunderland, and Roger Powell, also deserve thanks for their insight into the club scene, while fellow enthusiast Mike Costigan shared several dusty hours with me, trying to track down Herald competitions pictures.

There was also the search for pictorial record of the trans-Africa expedition, which started with Richard Bensted-Smith, and ended successfully with Howard Walker, and Maurice Rowe, of *Motor* magazine.

In their own individual ways, Michael Ware of the National Motor Museum, Bryan Kennedy of Connoisseur Carbooks, and T. G. Ragunathan (Standard Motor Products of India Ltd), all helped significantly, while I should also thank my good friends at *Autocar* magazine, for permission to quote so regularly, and so often, from their archives.

Finally, and it is *never* a case of 'last and least', my thanks to Richard Langworth, of New Hampshire, USA. Richard not only provided the complete chapter on the cars' American career, but is always around, on the end of the telephone, cryptically in print, or in person at least once a year, to keep me on the straight and narrow. Hindsight, they say, always helps judgement, but so, too, does distance. I need that Stateside perspective on so many issues.

Graham Robson

Burton Bradstock, Dorset
July 1985

Prologue

Although the Triumph Herald itself was new in many important respects, there was nothing new, at the time, in the concept of small Standards or small Triumphs being sold, for these had been on the scene, in Coventry, for generations. The Herald was first put on sale in 1959, but it was well-and-truly pre-dated by the stubby little Triumph Super Seven of 1927, while the original 'small Standard' was the very first car of all, the 6 hp model, of 1903!

It is important, even at this stage, to make it clear that the Standard, and Triumph, companies were quite independent of each other until 1944. The Triumph marque came into existence first of all, as a pedal cycle, then a motorcycle, though the original Triumph car was launched in 1923. The Standard was a new marque in 1903, with no lesser machines being built before that, to get the company on its feet.

Triumph's founder was Siegfried Bettman, in partnership with Mauritz Schulte, and long before the 10/20 hp car of 1923 was announced, Triumph motorcycles were famous. Company growth was steady, and it was not until 1927 that the 832 cc engined Super Seven was launched. Although the Super Seven was clearly influenced by the Austin Seven, it was quite different in detail, and sold very well. Over the years it grew up, and took on more power, but in the 1930s Triumph moved up-market, used Coventry-Climax engines for a time, and built a series of smart Glorias, Vitesses, and Dolomites.

Unfortunately, it was a bumpy financial ride, and finally the Triumph company (which had sold off the motorcycle business in 1936) descended into bankruptcy in 1939. After an inactive interregnum during the Second World War, under the ownership of Thos. Ward Ltd, a Sheffield-based engineering concern, the Triumph marque was taken over by the Standard Motor Co. Ltd towards the end of 1944. None of the Coventry factories, in which Triumph cars had once been made, were ever occupied by Standard, and a completely fresh start was made in 1946.

Standard began building cars in Much Park Street, Coventry, but the company expanded so rapidly that a move to Cash's Lane was followed by the start of a new complex, on undeveloped land, at Canley, which in those days was on the very outskirts of the city itself. The 9.5 hp Model 'S' was Standard's first volume-production small car, but it was the new Nine, announced at the same time as the Triumph Super Seven, which really set Standard on the way to rapid expansion.

Not only did the Nine form the basis of several other models in an expanding range, but Standard's founder, R. W. Maudslay, was joined by Captain John Black, as general manager, in 1929. In the next ten years Standard's output, from Canley, rocketed from less than 10,000 to more than 50,000 cars a

RIGHT ABOVE *One of the early 'small' Standards – this actually being the 9.9-hp 'Teignmouth' model of 1929, complete with fabric saloon, and artillery-style wheels*

RIGHT *In the 1920s, Triumph, still an independent company, produced the Super Seven, really in direct competition to the Austin Seven. This was a 1932-model two-seater*

year. During the 1930s there was always a 'Nine', a 'Little Nine' or a 'Big Nine' in the range, but from the autumn of 1938 the current Flying Standard line-up was rounded off by the all-new Flying Eight, which had a long-stroke 1,009 cc four-cylinder side valve engine.

There was very little time for the Flying Eight to establish itself before the Second World War—its engine, slightly enlarged, was also to be found in the Flying Nine, by the way, of 1937–39—but it was put back on sale in 1945 when the war was over. Out-moded or not, it sold very well indeed, and in the three years before it was dropped to make space for the post-war Vanguard to go into production, no fewer than 53,099 were built. Total production, including pre-war and war-time examples, had been 83,139.

By the end of the 1930s, Standard had produced a complete range of 'Flying' models – this being a 1939 example of the 1.0-litre Flying Eight tourer

Sir John Black (he had been knighted for his war-time efforts in industry) had, in the meantime, begun the transformation, and redevelopment of the Triumph marque. Described by some as ruthless, by others as a hard driver of men, and certainly a business dictator in all senses of the word, Sir John was not content with having dragged Standard up into 'membership' of Britain's 'Big Six' of car makers. Somehow, he still felt that there was more to be done. Not only did he want 'his' company to be bigger, but he also wanted it to have prestige as well.

During the 1930s he had become Standard's managing director, and in this period one of his most important deals was to arrange to sell engines, gearboxes and other mechanical components to William Lyons, who then produced his own rakish bodies to clothe them, and marketed them as SSs, or SS-Jaguars. After a time, this arrangement came to annoy the mercurial Capt. Black considerably, for SS-Jaguar (and William Lyons) were getting all

the praise, and the sporting image, though it was Standard who were providing much of the hardware.

Before the end of the 1930s, Capt. Black decided to ease Standard towards a more sporting image (the unsuccessful V8-engined 20 hp Flying Standard was one tentative move, the decision to supply chassis and running gear for the still-born Raymond Mays model another), and made a takeover offer to William Lyons. This was abruptly refused, and from that moment on, it seems, there was no love lost between the two tycoons.

Alick Dick, Sir John's young assistant towards the end of the war (he became Standard-Triumph's managing director in 1954, when Sir John made one too many dictatorial moves, and was ousted by his fellow

ABOVE *Captain John Black joined Standard, from Hillman, at the end of the 1920s, and became the company's managing director in the mid-1930s. Thereafter, he dictated the policy of the company, and made it into one of Britain's 'Big Six' car makers*

BELOW *The first post-war 'Standard-Triumph' saloon was the razor-edge 1800 of 1946, which used Flying Standard 14 mechanical components, and a Mulliner built bodyshell.* Not, *by any means, in the same price bracket as the Herald would later be!*

LEFT *Up to the early 1950s, all small Standard-Triumph engines were side-valve units. This was the Mayflower unit, itself directly descended from the Flying Nine unit of the 1930s*

RIGHT *This cutaway Mayflower, as prepared for public exhibition, shows the rather sit-up-and-beg style of the late 1940s. The Herald would have to be much sleeker than this!*

BELOW *The first small 'Standard-Triumph' was the Mayflower, announced in 1949, but not put on sale until mid-1950. Although this drawing shows a chassis, it was actually welded into place under the bodyshell on initial assembly. There were no future Herald components here, however – the engine was obsolescent Flying Standard type, while the gearbox and axle were Standard Vanguard based. The front suspension, new in itself, would later be used in the TR2 sports car*

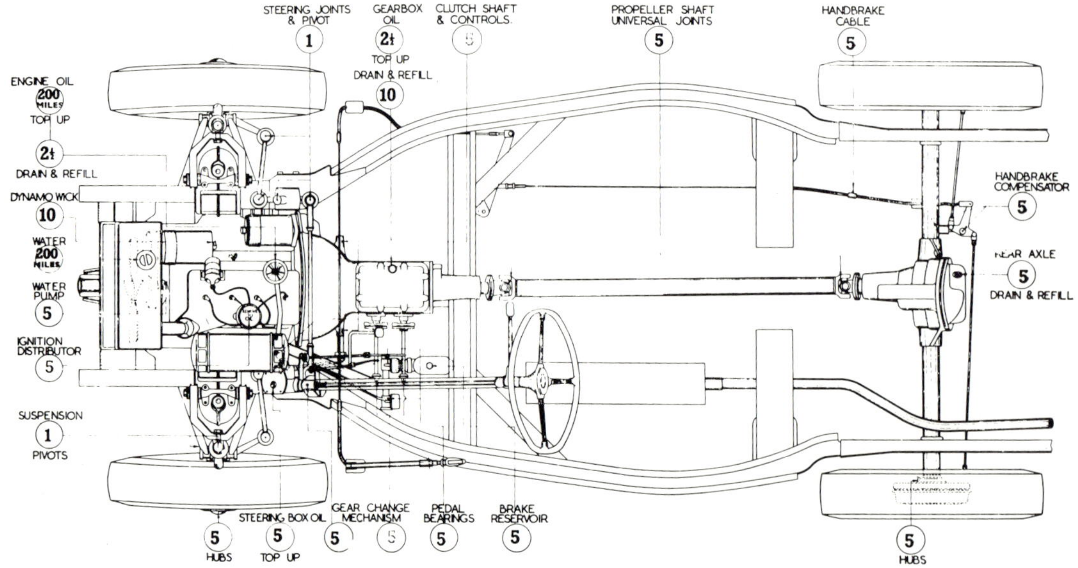

directors), recalls what then happened in 1944:

'. . . before the war Standard had been supplying parts to SS. Standard had special tooling for the six-cylinder engines, and for the overhead-valve version of the four-cylinder, of which Lyons took all supplies. Bill Lyons wanted to buy the tooling—he wanted to make all of his Jaguars in the future—and John Black was willing to let him have that so that we could build a competitive car. We kept the four-cylinder engine tooling, but it wasn't viable without a new chassis and a new name. So that's why we bought Triumph. Just because Bill Lyons made a sporting saloon, or a sports car. John Black was not going to let him get away with it!'

The buildings occupied by the rump of the Triumph company, in Coventry, had been plastered by German bombing in 1940, and no attempt was ever made to rescue the existing facilities, or to try to remanufacture parts. Most of the site, in fact, was bulldozed, and damaged machinery and parts sold as scrap. Nevertheless Alick Dick, along with Standard's chairman, Charles Band, recommended the purchase of the name, which was duly finalized in November 1944. Standard's director's minute book of 20 October 1944, comments as follows:

'Resolved that the action of the managing director in paying a deposit of £7,500 for the purchase by the company of the freehold property known as the Triumph works, Briton road, Coventry . . . including all finished and unfinished parts, together with the drawings and jigs and tools necessary for the manufacture of Triumph cars, including working drawings of engines, gearboxes and other parts, and together with the goodwill of the business, with the right to use the name Triumph in conjunction with any company to be registered by the Standard Motor Co. Ltd, be approved. . . . It was further resolved that the aforementioned premises . . . be purchased by the company at a cost of £75,000.'

But Sir John was only interested in the name (as this minute made clear), so he was not interested in retaining the bomb-damaged premises:

'We sold the factory to the B. O. Morris group for about the same amount,' Alick Dick recalled, 'and all we got was the name—for nothing—plus, I suppose, an obligation to supply spares for Triumph cars. But as there were hardly any of them, we really didn't feel any obligation to the old customers.'

Sir John, therefore, bore a healthy grudge against William Lyons, and was out to get even.

Alick Dick (left of group), and Sir John Black, inspecting one of the first production-built Mayflowers to be produced at Canley towards the end of June 1950

There was still time, however, for him to make one last attempt to come to terms with the Jaguar chairman. This was what Sir William Lyons later stated, in a 1969 speech:

'Sir John Black told me that he would no longer be able to make our engine, and after some discussion offered to sell to us the special plant he had put down for its production. . . . I had a great admiration for John Black in many respects, but I quickly grasped the opportunity to obtain security. Therefore, within a few days, I sent transport to collect the plant and sent our cheque in payment for it. It turned out that I had been right to do so for it was not long before Black proposed that we should revert to the previous arrangement and return the plant to Standard. He pressed me very hard, even to the extent of suggesting that we should form a separate company together. . . .'

Whereupon Sir John Black set out to create a new 'Triumph' marque, to compete directly with Jaguar. If only he had known that William Lyons and his small engineering team were already planning to produce a sensational new range of cars powered by the excellent twin-cam XK engine he might not have bothered. As it was, however, Sir John wanted to match cars like the $1\frac{1}{2}$-litre Jaguar 'Mk IV' and the $2\frac{1}{2}$-litre models, with rivals that his own engineers would create. To do this without the same backing and flair of a genius for styling like Lyons himself was foolhardy in the extreme. Even though Standard now employed Walter Belgrove, who had been Triumph's chief body engineer in the mid and late 1930s, they would have to fight an uphill battle.

In terms of sales, the first phase to re-establish a Triumph marque was only partly successful. In March 1946, the company announced a pair of new models—the 1800 Roadster, and the 1800 Town and Country saloon—both based on cheap-to-build tubular chassis frames, but with suspensions, engine and all running gear from the existing Standard Flying 14. The Roadster was styled by Frank Callaby, and the saloon mainly by Mulliners of Birmingham, with some retouching by Walter Belgrove.

These cars were neither quick enough, nimble enough, nor distinguished enough to make much of an impression on Jaguar, and after the XK-engined 120 sports car and Mk VII saloons arrived it was 'no contest'. All in all,

Sideways assembly of Mayflowers was a feature to become familiar with the small Standards, and the Heralds, which followed them later in the 1950s. This shot, of course, was taken in the old Canley assembly hall, in the summer of 1950

between 1946 and 1954, a total of 4,501 Roadsters, and 15,491 saloons of several sub-derivatives, were produced.

Nothing daunted, therefore, Sir John changed tack again. (There was nothing new in this, in the late 1940s—he seemed to do it more and more often, at times without obvious reason!) This time he would produce a rather up-market small car, using the Triumph name, and he would use it to spearhead an export drive, to North America. It was certainly with North America in mind that he caused it to be named the Triumph Mayflower. The bare bones of the project, if not its name, had been settled as early as 1944, when Standard announced the purchase of Triumph, and that they intended to produce a new '10 hp' model.

It was, in fact, the only new small car that Standard-Triumph were developing at this time. Even so, it took a long time to turn a bright idea into cars for sale in the showrooms. The Mayflower was not unveiled until October 1949, and even this launch was premature. Series production did not begin until June/July 1950, nearly six years after the '10 hp' model had first been mentioned.

There were many good reasons for this. On the one hand, there was such a pent-up demand for new models, and the body tooling they required, that everyone, mighty or humble, had to get into a queue for facilities at one or other of the companies. On the other, Standard-Triumph were heavily pre-occupied, at first, with the build-up of tractor production at the Banner Lane factory, on behalf of Harry Ferguson.

At first, and until 1948, production at Canley concentrated on the revived, pre-war type, Standard Flying Eights, Twelves and Fourteens, along with the tubular-framed Triumph Roadsters and Saloons which I have already mentioned. Then, from the spring of that year, came the bulbous but profitable Standard

Sir John Black posing with a Mayflower – a car of which he was very proud, even though it had very controversial, traditional, styling

Vanguard. It was only then that the next new car could be made ready.

Project 1200T (the 'T', clearly, stood for Triumph) was on the stocks by 1947, but a batch of prototypes were not built until 1949, and all had that well-known, if not universally-liked, razor edge body style. Because Standard-Triumph still had no body-building facilities of their own, a typically complex Sir John Black deal resulted in Mulliners of Birmingham styling the 84 in. wheelbase car, and the still-independent company of Fisher & Ludlow (of Birmingham and Tile Hill, Coventry) building them in quantity!

Under its skin, the 1200T car had a Vanguard gearbox and a Vanguard back axle, but its own particular brand of independent front suspension which would later find a home in the Triumph TR2 sports car. The engine was an improved version of the pre-war Flying Ten unit, with side valves, 1,247 cc, and 38 bhp (gross). There was one notable innovation, in that the car had no separate chassis frame. In fact there was a separate perimeter-type frame at first, but this was channel-section and open-topped, and permanently welded to the body floor during assembly at Fisher & Ludlow. In crude terms, therefore, this *was* a chassisless body structure, the very first to be used on a Standard-Triumph car.

Although 35,000 Mayflowers were built in three years, it was probably not a profitable model for the company, and all ideas of modernizing it, with overhead valve engine conversions, were abandoned. All in all, it was neither cheap, good-looking, nor lively enough to please enough people. It did Standard-Triumph's reputation for building small cars no good at all, and it certainly was not a small 'Triumph' by traditional standards.

Now it was time to start again, and this time the new car would *have* to be good.

LEFT *Some Mayflowers looked better than others! This gleaming example was owned, for a time, by American Triumph historian, Richard Langworth*

ABOVE *The very rare Mayflower drop-head coupé, which was modified by Mulliners from a saloon shell supplied by Fisher & Ludlow. Once again, not a shape that the Herald convertible would emulate!*

Chapter 1
Standard 8, 10 and Pennant: laying the foundations

Work to replace the Mayflower began as soon as the first production cars were made, though it was not until November 1950 that it was agreed that a completely new car would be necessary. From this point, as the 'SC' (=Small Car) project began to take shape, the first events which influenced the birth, and the anatomy, of the Herald, also took place. Without SC, in fact, the Herald could not have been built, for its engine, gearbox and back axle were all derived from those designed for SC in the early 1950s.

Herald enthusiasts, however, should be grateful that 'SC' was not put on sale in the form originally envisaged! In the beginning, it might even have been a rear-engined car (the company inspected a Renault 4CV very carefully at the time—for the 4CV was the 'fashionable' new design of the day), and in summer 1951 it was still evolving around the chassis/floorpan of the Mayflower, with a new small side-valve engine, and a three-speed gearbox without synchromesh. At all costs, it seems, Sir John Black was determined to get the costs right down, the reason being that the Austin A30, also new from stem to stern, was to sell for a mere £507, with four-door coachwork, while the Mayflower was selling for £655. For a mere £519, too, one could buy a four-door Morris Minor.

The problem was that although Standard-Triumph's chief chassis design engineer, Harry Webster, was a fast driver, and a motoring enthusiast, his technical director, Ted Grinham, was not. To the grim and stolid Grinham, motoring was not for fun, but for transportation, and a car of which he was particularly proud—the Standard Vanguard—proves his point, and his philosophy!

In a way, we can all thank Austin's chairman Len Lord, and the A30, for the eventual form of 'SC', for it was immediately after this car had gone on show at Earls Court in 1951 that SC began to take on its familiar form. By January 1952 it had been agreed that the car should have an all-new engine of between 750 and 800 cc, with overhead valve gear (though the side-valve engines originally proposed would be built for testing to start, then discarded when ohv units followed them), and that it should have an all-new unit-construction body/chassis unit.

The first car's body was built at Coventry, with assistance from Fisher & Ludlow, and all design details were settled by mid-1952, except that Sir John Black himself finally chose a four-speed box, when a three-speeder was still being discussed at the end of 1952. The Mayflower engine plant was converted to build the new small engines, as a temporary measure, but permanent, advanced, transfer-line machinery was ordered, and would finally be ready for use by the spring of 1955.

In many ways, SC followed the A30, for the engine was of almost exactly the same size (though it had a much more promising cylinder head casting, as far as breathing was concerned), though the SC had a 4.5 in. longer wheelbase and weighed 150 lb more than the Austin. The A30 body structure, however, was 'home-made' at Longbridge, whereas SC was to be produced by Fisher & Ludlow, along with

ABOVE *Standard's board of directors in the late 1950s, when the 'Zobo' project got the go-ahead. Lord Tedder, company chairman, is at the head of the table, near the camera, with his managing director, Alick Dick, to his right*

LEFT *Engineering director, Ted Grinham, who was Alick Dick's deputy in the mid-1950s, headed the team which conceived the 'SC' project. He retired before the Herald design was finalized*

ODU 830

STA
57

LEFT *The original 'SC', or Standard Eight, of 1953, was a dumpy little saloon car, of monocoque construction, with an 803 cc overhead valve engine. This was the engine which, later developed, would power the forthcoming Herald*

LEFT BELOW *By the spring of 1957, when design of the Herald was beginning, the Standard Eight had become more civilized, complete with winding rather than sliding windows, and with an opening boot lid. In style, and layout, however, the Herald would be a quantum leap forward*

RIGHT *Compare this with the later Herald engine! This was the original 803 cc unit of 1954 vintage, with a single downdraught carburettor . . .*

BELOW *. . . and this was the coil spring independent front suspension of the 'SC' Standard Eight, once again similar, but by no means the same, as that of the later Herald. Note, in particular, the number of grease nipples on this assembly*

the existing Standard Vanguard, and directly replacing the Triumph Mayflower.

The most controversial feature of the car was its equipment—or, rather, the lack of it. In its initial form the dumpy little four-seater saloon was so sparse that Sir John Black dubbed it 'Belsen' (after the World War 2 concentration camp, and the very under-nourished inhabitants contained therein). The original car, now called Standard 8, was launched in September 1953, had a simple body style, a radiator air intake unadorned by any type of grille, sliding windows in the doors, and no external access to the boot lid. The rear seats were thinly padded, and could be somersaulted forward to give access to the boot itself.

All of which, Standard-Triumph thought, was fully justified by the price of £481, which brought it on to the market cheaper than the existing A30 (£504 for the four-door) and the Morris Minor Series II (£557 for the four-door).

The engine was all new, with a simple but rugged design, and it had a cast-iron cylinder block, a cast-iron head with six ports (the inlet ports were siamezed), and a three-bearing crankshaft. There was a single downdraught Solex 26 ZIACO curburettor, with the inlet and exhaust manifolds being cast together, with a permanent hot spot between the two.

Bore, stroke and capacity were 58 × 76 mm, 803 cc, which was exactly the same as the BMC A-Series unit used in the A30 and the Morris Minor (though BMC claimed the capacity as 800 cc!). Peak power was 26 bhp (net) at 4500 rpm, peak torque 39 lb. ft at 2800 rpm. It was a very modest start—but as we now know, there was a great deal of extra development still to come.

The Standard Eight of 1954 still had sliding windows, and no exterior boot access, but the Ten which followed it had 'proper' winding windows, and a chrome grille to decorate the front air intake

The first twin-SU engine for the 'SC' engine was produced by Alexander Engineering, of Haddenham, in Bucks, and was made optional on the Ten. Many details would be changed before a Triumph-designed twin-carb installation was produced for the Herald

The gearbox, too, was all-new, with four speeds, and synchromesh on top, third and second gears. Change was by a long and rather willowy central lever, and the clutch was a 6.25 in. single-dry-plate unit. There was a new, small, hypoid bevel back axle, with 39 ring teeth and an eight-tooth pinion, which gave a ratio of 4.875:1. The differential was located in a banjo casing, with a bolt-on nose-piece. Overall ratios were 4.875, 7.088, 11.993, 20.82, and reverse also 20.81:1.

Six months later, by which time assembly of Standard 8s was in full-scale production at Canley (and where final assembly took place with the cars being mounted sideways on the moving track), the much more attractive Standard 10 was announced. This derivative had been planned right from the start, and 300 a day of both types could be built.

The Ten was really the Eight with all the penny-pinching ideas discarded, and with substantially more performance than before. The enlarged engine had, in fact, been installed in the second prototype of all, the design and the production tooling always having taken account of this stretch.

The engine itself was, quite simply, a bored out version of the 803 cc unit, having a 63 mm bore instead of 58 mm, a capacity of 948 cc and peak figures of 33 bhp at 4500 rpm; 46 lb ft torque at 2500 rpm. Incidentally, Standard-Triumph beat BMC to this engine size by well over two years—BMC did not follow suit until the autumn of 1956. The Standard Ten's carburettor was a Solex 26ZIS, and there were larger valves, modified chambers, and other minor changes to the manifolding.

The gearbox was that of the Eight, but the back axle ratio was changed, there being 41 ring teeth, nine pinion teeth, and a ratio of 4.55:1. Both this, and the original 4.875:1 ratio, would become familiar to Herald owners in the years to come.

Visually, and in its equipment, the Ten was much changed. At the front there was a simple pressed grille around the air intake, the doors all had winding windows, and there was external access to the boot by a lift-up boot lid. The car's interior was much more completely trimmed and furnished, the seats had Dunlopillo casings, and the rear seats did not fold forward, as access to the boot was no longer needed. The price—£581—was still attractive, and sales surged ahead.

Nothing trendy, certainly from this angle, in the Standard Ten of 1954!

Company finances benefited accordingly, as this simple profits table confirms:

1952 £530,631 after taxation
1953 £644,330 after taxation
1954 £886,259 after taxation
1955 £1,934,044 after taxation

Some of this improvement, of course, was also attributable to the buoyant state of tractor sales, and to the growing reputation of the TR2 sports car.

By this time, too, there had been personnel upheavals, right at the top, of the Standard Motor Co. Ltd. Sir John Black, having become more and more dictatorial in recent years, was ousted in a boardroom coup in January 1954, and his assistant, Alick Dick, took over as managing director. Ted Grinham, already technical director, became Alick Dick's deputy, and from the middle of 1954 Lord Tedder (who had been a famous RAF chief during the Second World War) became the company's chairman.

There was more to come. In the summer of 1955, a charismatic ex-Ford UK staff man, Martin Tustin, was appointed as a director, and general manager, and from the spring of 1957 Harry Webster moved up to become director of engineering, after Ted Grinham retired. It is not over-stating the case to suggest that Standard-Triumph cars began to become more sporting almost from that point, and that the original 'Zobo' or Triumph Herald, project began to take shape from then.

The badging on this car says 'Triumph 10', in which guise the Standard Ten was exported to several territories in the 1950s. Mechanically the two types were identical

ABOVE *In the UK it was the Standard Companion, but overseas it was often a Triumph Companion – the chunky but versatile estate car produced on the basis of the 'SC' design*

RIGHT ABOVE *As an interim step, while decisions were being made about a brand new car, the company produced the Standard Pennant, which was a drastically face-lifted Standard Ten, with new front and rear wings. Somehow, though, it looked higher and narrower, even than before*

RIGHT *From the rear the Pennant, which was* not *styled by Michelotti, had embryo tail fins. Michelotti would do this in a much more elegant manner for 1959*

In the next few years, Standard-Triumph's sales force never seemed to leave well alone. Although the basic shape and style of the cars did not change, more and yet more sub-derivatives, and options, were launched to make the cars as attractive as possible. Soon after the Ten arrived, an Eight De Luxe was put on sale, with wind-up windows and more complete trim, and within a year the 'basic' Eight became 'Family Eight' with similar improvements. In the meantime the estate car version of this shell (with body by Mulliners Ltd) had been produced, and originally called 'Good Companion' before settling down to be called, simply, 'Companion'.

For 1956 there were the 'Super Eight' and 'Super Ten' models, which were further improved in terms of trim and finish, and in March of that year came the Family Ten—a cross between the no-boot-lid body and the Ten's engine and drive line.

STA 58

There was more to come. In September 1956, Standard followed the craze for 'two-pedal-control', which meant getting rid of the clutch pedal; their particular system, called 'Standrive', was produced by Newton & Bennett, who would soon become a Standard-Triumph subsidiary. More important was the move, in March 1957, to make the new small Laycock overdrive optional on Eights and Tens. For £63.75, factory-fitted when the cars were new, overdrive could be operated on top, third and second gears, giving a seven-speed transmission in which several effective ratios seemed to overlap!

Finally, the lack of boot lid on certain versions was rectified when, from April 1957, the latest cars not only had an opening boot lid, but a rather cheap and cheerful grille across the radiator air intake, and an up-rated engine (as powerful as the 'Ten' unit) which offered 33 bhp (net) at 5000 rpm. This was known as the Gold Star unit.

In the meantime, Alexander engineering had produced a very effective twin SU engine and chassis conversion for the Standard Eight and Ten, which Jimmy Ray's 'works' Ten, entered as a modified, or 'Grand Touring' machine, had used so successfully to win the RAC International Rally of March 1955. Before the end of that year the factory had decided to make the 'Hi-Power' kit an officially approved conversion, without this affecting the car's warranty. For about £62, which included the engine kit, an axle ratio change, and a front anti-roll bar, the enthusiast could have a sporty little 37 bhp Eight, or a 42 bhp Ten. Many considered this to be very good value and—looking back, with the benefit of hindsight—it seems to have encouraged Standard-Triumph's own engineers to develop a similar installation for future Heralds and Spitfires.

Then, in October 1957, came the only major facelift to which this basic bodyshell was ever treated; a new model which had been developed as something of an 'interim' car, to tide over the range until something entirely fresh could be produced and which was at one time to have been called 'Triumph Mayflower', was finally revealed as the Standard Pennant.

One feature of the Pennant, retained from earlier 'SCs' was the fold down rear seat. This would be available on early Heralds, too

In simple terms, the Pennant was an up-market version of the Ten, with new front end and rear end styling, a new facia layout, and generally upgraded trim and fittings. There were new front wings, with hooded headlamps, and new rear wings with protruding tail lamp clusters. The capital expenditure on this retooling had been a mere £125,000, though an extra £100,000 for a two-door version had been vetoed by the board of directors.

Mechanically, the Pennant was almost pure Standard Ten, except that the engine had been upgraded, with a 28 mm Solex carburettor and an 8.0:1 compression ratio, to produce 37 bhp (net) at 5000 rpm. Two-pedal control, and overdrive, were also available, and most cars were built with a two-tone colour scheme, the upper and lower shades being separated by a rather arbitrarily-aligned plated strip.

For the Pennant of October 1957, Standard-Triumph produced a neat facia and instrument style which, frankly, was nicer than the Herald style which followed two years later. Does the steering wheel look familiar?

The most significant improvement was that the long gear lever of the Standard Ten had been discarded, and in its place was a neat, short, and stubby gearlever, much further back than before, connected to the box by a remote control linkage. Herald/Vitesse enthusiasts should realize, however, that the Pennant's remote change has nothing at all in common with their cars, for lever and pivot was directly attached to the transmission tunnel, with an exposed link to a unique selector 'tower' atop the gearbox casing.

It is interesting, now, to look back at the Pennant, its price relative to its rivals, and to where it fitted in the market place. By 1958, when it was in full production, it had to face up to competition from Ford and BMC, all of whose cars were significantly better than ever before. Britain's motor industry, in fact, was booming, and competition at this level was intense. Here are the details:

Model	Engine size/power	Total UK price
Standard Pennant	948/37 bhp	£729
(Standard Super Ten)	948/37 bhp	£654
Austin A35 four-door (de Luxe)	948/34 bhp	£601
Ford Prefect (de Luxe)	1172/36 bhp	£658
Morris Minor 1000 four-door (de Luxe)	948/34 bhp	£694

The Pennant's 948 cc engine and transmission of 1957, now very close in design and detail to what would follow for the Herald. There was, of course, much more vertical space under the bonnet of the Pennant, which explains how such a big air cleaner canister could be employed

The Pennant, therefore, was already more expensive than all its rivals, but it had several potential sales advantages over all of them. Compared with the Ford, Austin or Morris products, it was the only one to offer overdrive or two-pedal control options—though it must be admitted that 'two-pedal control' was only a passing fad that did little except keep warranty and service staffs busy in future years.

The Autocar tested an overdrive Pennant in February 1958, fitted with the overdrive option (£63.75) and duo-tone paintwork (£11.25), radio (£28.50) and a heater (£19.50), all of which gave it a ready-to-go price of £851.85, a considerable sum for a 948 cc engined, 11 ft 10 in. long saloon car.

The car's maximum speed was almost the same in three different gears—66 mph in direct top, or overdrive third, and 64 mph in overdrive top! The power output claimed for the 948 cc engine must still have been somewhat optimistic, especially when one considers that 0–60 mph took no less than 34.9 sec, and the standing start quarter mile 25.0 sec. Overall fuel consumption, however, was excellent at 39.6 mpg.

The Pennant, of course, was by no means a light car (the test car weighed 1745 lb), and the aerodynamics of that bluff-nosed bodyshell must have been rather awful. Not only that, but all its rivals were significantly quicker than this, and only the side-valve engined Ford Prefect was less economical. Yet, for all that, Ken Richardson's 'works' Pennants took second and third places, overall, in the snowy RAC Rally of March 1958, behind Peter Harper's Sunbeam Rapier.

When the last of these passenger cars was built in November 1959, however, there was no

The 'electrical' side of the 948 cc Pennant engine, so similar in so many ways to the Herald unit. The gear selector housing, and the gearbox/body mountings, however, are completely different

doubt that the project had been a huge financial success. Not only were there the cars already described above, but there were 'Triumph' badged derivatives for certain export markets, including the United States, vans and pickups, the small commercial vehicles actually being built until the mid-1960s, well after the Herald range had reached maturity.

Individual production totals were as follows:

Standard Eight (all versions)	136,317
Standard Ten (all versions)	172,500
Standard Pennant	42,910
Triumph Ten (export only)	9907
Triumph Estate wagon (export only 'Companion')	7351
Triumph Pennant (export only)	335

By 1959, though, the SC family had been made obsolete, by cars of the Zobo family, which we now know as the Triumph Heralds. Not only the layout of the new car itself, but its marque name, were different and there had been a great deal of aggravation, not only in settling on a viable design, but in finding suitable sources of supply. Even so, many mechanical developments finalized for the Ten and the Pennant were also of vital importance to the new Heralds. All in all, Zobo would probably not have brought in on time, at the right price, without the invaluable experience, and production, of the previous machines.

Chapter 2
'Zobo' and Michelotti: the Italian connection

Long before the Standard 8 and 10 hp family had paid off its investment in tooling, Standard-Triumph's directors had started to consider ways of replacing it. SC, as a design, and a style, was good, but not that good. It was making money for the company, but it was hardly making much of a reputation. So, what to do next?

There was no established product planning department at Standard-Triumph at the time. Before Sir John Black had moved out, he had made all the big decisions, often in a most capricious way, and after that major new models seemed to evolve as a result of talks between Alick Dick, Martin Tustin, and Ted Grinham.

They were very different, in character and in outlook. Alick Dick was the 'Young Turk', the rather glamorous businessman just as ready to sell his company to a wealthy partner as to underpin it for a steady but unspectacular future. Martin Tustin was the dynamic, ex-Ford general manager, a great enthusiast, always wanting to drive prototypes and get involved in engineering, and always pushing ahead rapidly, wanting instant action. Ted Grinham could not have been more different. He was an older man, ultra-cautious, very dour, and not really interested in motor cars for enjoyment, but merely for transportation. Harry Webster, still young, a fast and skilful driver, and lover of sports cars and motor sport, was Grinham's deputy, but still 'in the wings', as it were.

In the spring of 1956, the executive (i.e. non-Board) directors were already giving consideration 'to the tooling up early in 1958 for a completely new 8/10 hp range, for introduction at the 1958 Motor Show'. In the meantime, however, the existing car was to be restyled as an interim measure, and this project eventually came to maturity as the Standard Pennant, introduced in October 1957, and built until June 1960 in a variety of guises.

At this time, it seems, Standard-Triumph had every intention of producing their car with a conventional, unit-construction, body/chassis unit, following on their current experience with the SC models, and with the Standard Vanguard III. Then, in corporate terms, the roof fell in. Specifically, Alick Dick discovered that he could not find a major supplier willing, or able, to provide tooling and manufacturing facilities to build the bodyshells for his new car!

The problem was that Standard-Triumph, like Rootes, Jaguar, Rover and Rolls-Royce, had no unique facilities of their own for producing bodyshells in quantity, before the mid-1950s, and had to rely on the services of a major supplier like Fisher & Ludlow, or Pressed Steel Co.

Up until 1953, Standard-Triumph had been able to rely on Fisher & Ludlow, who had factories in Birmingham, and at Tile Hill, just a couple of miles from the Canley factory. Way back in the 1930s, F & L had opened the Tile Hill plant with long-term, high-volume, Standard business in mind. F & L had provided bodies for the Flying Standard Eight, for the Triumph Mayflower which followed it, and for the SC Standard 8s and 10s which the Herald was to displace.

A familiar picture, but nonetheless important. Seen at the launch party for the new Herald are (left) Harry Webster, who masterminded the design, (centre) Giovanni Michelotti, the talented Italian who styled and partly engineered the bodyshell, and (right) Martin Tustin, the company's general manager, who saw it put into production, and who also oversaw the building of the vast new assembly hall

However, in the early 1950s the new BMC group, lead by the forceful Leonard Lord, and numbering Austin, Morris, Wolseley and several other marques among its assets, began to expand even more. In August 1953, just before volume production of the Standard 8 hp saloon got under way, BMC launched a successful bid for control of Fisher & Ludlow, and, as *The Motor* then commented: 'If the BMC offer goes through, the Pressed Steel Co. of Oxford will be the only large-scale independent motor-body producer in Britain.'

Standard-Triumph's immediate reaction had been to award the contract for tooling and pressing the monocoque Vanguard Phase III to Pressed Steel (the first of these cars was built in the autumn of 1955), and soon after this an exclusivity agreement was concluded with Mulliners Ltd, of Birmingham, which guaranteed this independent concern's allegiance to Standard-Triumph as soon as existing contracts (to build shells such as the Aston Martin DB2/4, for instance) could be wound up.

In the meantime, however, Alick Dick hoped that existing links with Fisher & Ludlow could be maintained, especially as the Tile Hill factory was so close by. The fact that a categorical assurance regarding continuity of SC body supply was received from Arthur Keats of Fisher & Ludlow seemed to make this all the more likely.

But all was not what it seemed. When Alick Dick discussed the matter with Sir Leonard

ABOVE *Webster was never serious about this, but at least he assessed the possibility of making a separate chassis using tubes! It would neither have been strong enough, nor cheap enough. This dates from February 1957, incidentally*

BOTH ABOVE *Early in 1957, Standard-Triumph were in despair over the style for 'Zobo', and this model shows the 'bathtub on wheels' shape that was slowly evolving. Everyone hated it, and without a figurehead chief stylist at the factory since Walter Belgrove had left in 1955, there was no inspiration to do better. Soon after this fate, in the shape of Raymond Flower, and his young Italian protégé, stepped in*

Lord of BMC, which now controlled Fisher & Ludlow, Sir Leonard bluntly told him 'to push off'. (I dare not print the actual words used, according to Alick Dick—Sir Leonard could be very crude when the mood took him!) Having ascertained that Dick required tooling capacity for a new car which would presumably compete directly with his own Austin A30, he refused categorically to consider the business.

(In fact, though logical, this was cutting off Fisher & Ludlow's nose to spite its face, for when the SC contract came to an end, the Tile Hill factory had no more business, and had to be sold off. The new owners, eventually, were . . . Standard Triumph!)

Nothing daunted, Alick Dick then turned to Pressed Steel, which was supplying many customers, and was horrified to discover that there was a big queue for their services from the booming British motor industry, and that no tooling expertise would be available for some considerable time. If only he had known what was involved, Dick would have seen that he had to queue behind Rootes, for the new Husky and a light commercial vehicle, behind Rover for the P5 3-litre saloon, behind BMC themselves for the Austin-Healey Sprite sports car, *and* for the first of the B-Series Farina saloons!

RIGHT ABOVE *When Standard-Triumph invited Michelotti to produce a new style for the TR3 sports car, he evolved this startling shape, and Vignale built a shell, all in the space of three months, in the spring of 1957*

RIGHT *The tail of the Michelotti TR3 dream car had pronounced tail fins, and a squared-off mass around the bumpers. Both front and rear themes would figure, in due course, in the Herald which followed. The models on the wall were all of possible facelifts for the Standard Vanguard III – and Michelotti was already tackling that job by the summer of 1957!*

This was an enormous problem, and it brought the new project to a halt for many months. One result was that it made Alick Dick even more anxious to merge Standard with another partner (on the 'Safety in Numbers' principle)—the company had joined in merger talks with Rover in 1954, would talk to Rootes in 1957, Massey Harris Ferguson in the same year, and Rover once again in 1959. The other was that it made him determined, somehow, to become less reliant on outside suppliers, even though he had very good relations with Sankeys, who not only supplied chassis frames, but were expanding their body presswork facility, in the hope of capturing new business for the 1960s.

Everything which followed in the next few years had an influence on the layout, and the form, of the Herald. In the spring of 1956, Standard had made a successful takeover bid for Beans Industries, of the West Midlands, whose principal expertise was in producing castings. This was done, originally, to secure casting supplies for tractor components, but

LEFT *The first Standard-Triumph independent rear suspension, built as a production design, was for the Herald, but at the same time, the engineers also found time to produce this system for the TR3. The picture dates from December 1957, half-elliptic leaf springs were still used, along with a modified 'live-axle' chassis frame, but there were new pressed steel 'bridges' to support the differential, and the lever-arm dampers. Fascinating!*

LEFT BELOW *By November 1957, the chassis design of 'Zobo' was taking its near-final shape. No pictures of the original transverse leaf spring front end survive, but this is probably one of the first coil spring frames. Students of Herald frame layouts, however, will realise that there are many detail differences . . .*

BELOW . . . *particularly at the front, where the pick-up points and supports for the independent front suspension are very spindly, and not at all as 'elegant' as the production design would become*

would eventually be of great value when new projects like the in-line six-cylinder engine, and the revised (all-synchromesh) gearbox casing came along.

Then, in the spring of 1958, Standard made a full-blooded bid for control for Mulliners Ltd, who themselves had controlled Forward Radiator since 1957. Although this body-building concern was very resourceful, and very versatile, it did not have the ultra-heavy press tool capacity to produce chassisless underpans, and its main use for the factory would be in producing separate shells (like the TR3A, which it was already building), major modifications of other shells (such as the Companion estate car completion of a Fisher & Ludlow, part-built, saloon car shell), or in producing major sections for other branches of the firm.

There was more to come. Relations between Standard, and Massey Harris Ferguson (on whose behalf they had been building Ferguson tractors for some years) had deteriorated steadily since Sir John Black resigned, and this culminated in an unwanted takeover offer in 1957, and interference in the Mulliners transaction in 1958. Alick Dick resolved to unscramble Standard from the tractor-building deal as soon as possible, and this was done during the summer of 1959. One result of this was that Standard gained about £12.5 million in cash, and had new capital with which to go shopping for more suppliers.

With this in mind, Alick Dick and Ken Aspland negotiated with the Ministry of Supply for the lease of a 297,000 sq ft factory at Radford, Coventry (hard by the Daimler Co.'s premises), which they originally thought might be used for the introduction of car paint and trim facilities. By the time the lease was finalized, however, it had been decided to turn Radford into a dedicated transmissions machining centre, which would release a lot of space at Canley for assembly purposes.

Later in 1959, too, the Alford & Alder business, from Hemel Hempstead, which produced front suspension and steering gear for the company, and Hall Engineering (Holdings) Ltd, of Liverpool, which not only built body pressings and sub-assemblies, but which also owned the very resourceful tooling concern of Auto Body Dies Ltd, was also swept into the fold.

It was not the sum total of the race for self-sufficiency, which Alick Dick, and Standard, carried out in the late 1950s, and I will be returning to this somewhat later. In the meantime, the search for the right sort of vehicle design continued. Not only was this all going to be dependent on the eventual source of bodyshell, or monocoque, supply but there was prolonged discussion about the very type of car it actually ought to be.

In fairness to Alick Dick and his colleagues, the new project could not possibly have come along at a worse time in the company's history. First, there was the fact that Ted Grinham was running up to retirement (he set this date for the end of 1956), and second was the economic condition of the country, and world-wide markets.

Ted Grinham had given long and honourable service to Standard—he had been appointed chief engineer in 1931, and had joined the board of directors in 1936—but there was no doubt that he was a very conventional thinker, who influenced the production of conventional, even boring, cars. The clear evidence of this is in cars like the Standard Vanguards, the Mayflower, and the SC range. Ex-chief body engineer Walter Belgrove once told me that he had no interest in anything sporting, and that the famous TR2 sports car took shape almost independently of him.

The inference, borne out by events, is that the new small car which Grinham wanted to build was not the car which his successor, Harry Webster, would want, and I have no doubt that

ABOVE *This November 1957 shot also shows the early type of 'Zobo' rear end, and independent suspension location. In particular, there was a big bridge across the nose of the differential casing, which was itself quite different from the production layout. The frame's rear end, too, has a quite different shape*

LEFT *November 1957, and the front suspension is fitted to a prototype frame. Note, at this stage, the use of disc brakes, but no evidence of an anti-roll bar* the Herald as we know it would never have been produced if Grinham had still been in control of design and development. It also meant that the project studies for the car, which took place in 1956, were all rendered obsolete in 1957.

1956 was also the year in which Britain's booming economy went sharply into reverse for a short time, as government applied a credit squeeze. In 1955, the British motor industry had produced 897,560 cars, while in 1956 this plunged to 707,594, and one result was that most of the large companies had to resort to short-time working to reduce their production. Another result was that profits were hit very badly—at Standard the after-tax figure plunged from £1,934,044 in 1955, to £573,004 in 1956, and down to no more than £419,925 in 1957.

(There was to be a big recovery in 1958, to £1,003,582, but part of this was due to the absorption of the profitable Mulliners group.)

But this was not all. In November 1956 the Arab-Israeli war erupted along the Suez canal, British and French troops intervened, the canal itself was blocked for a time, and oil supplies to Europe were speedily disrupted. Not only did petrol prices rise sharply, but the British government imposed rationing on 17 December 1956; this was not lifted until May 1957.

Naturally, most of the big firms rushed to consider the building of super-economy cars, and Standard was one of them. While the existing Standard 8s and 10s were already well-respected for their fuel efficiency, it was thought that further improvements could be made. John Lloyd confirms that first thoughts were to develop a light, ultra-cheap, ultra-economical new car. There was even talk of chasing that elusive Holy Grail of European motoring—to produce a car with a maximum speed of 60 mph, but overall fuel consumption of 60 mpg. It wasn't possible then, and it is still not done today, nearly 30 years later!

The problem of body supply, however, loomed over everything else. No matter which way the company turned, it was clear that they could not secure tooling, and mass-production supply (3000 a week) of unit-construction body/chassis units by the end of 1958. This was a target which Alick Dick was not going to let slip, so if Standard could not wait any longer than this, an alternative solution was needed.

The only feasible alternative was to step back a few years, look sideways at what was being done in the commercial vehicle industry, and design a car around a separate chassis. Not only that, but it was necessary to consider buying in the bodyshell in sections. As Harry Webster said, in an interview not long ago:

'We had to devise a car which was designed in such a way that its body components could be produced in various locations and then come together like parts of a jigsaw . . . you might say we were making a virtue out of a necessity but the idea also appealed (to us) on export grounds. When we sent the car abroad in CKD (Completely Knocked Down—or "kit") form, it could be easily assembled with the chassis acting as a jig for correctly locating the various body components.'

It might have been 'a virtue out of a necessity', but it was an extremely resourceful move which, as far as I can tell, was never copied by any other concern in the private-car business. You might say that Land-Rovers, and light commercial vehicles, were also built up in this way, but there was no private-car precedent on which to draw.

In the light of subsequent events, it was also an (unconscious) stroke of genius, for it allowed a great variety of derivatives—saloons, coupés, convertibles, estate cars, and vans, plus a one-off pick-up—all to be produced with the minimum tooling investment. It is also highly unlikely that a six-cylinder version could ever have been produced if a conventional unit construction monocoque had been chosen, complete with expensively tooled front panels and cross-members.

Even so, the problems were not over. First, the right type of separate chassis frame had to be produced (and cost targets were very tight . . .), and secondly there was the problem of developing an acceptable style. The chassis dilemma was solved relatively quickly but the styling problem rumbled on and on. The company was in trouble.

John Lloyd, who had come to manage the chassis test and experimental department in 1956, while it was still located at Banner Lane (the huge Government 'shadow factory' which Standard were using to produce tractors for Ferguson), told me that the very first experimental frame for the new project was actually an angle-iron space frame: 'Yes, really,' he insists, 'but it wasn't very good!' I should think not—nor, it seems, was a further attempt to produce a multi-tube frame much more successful. That, at least, might have been more structurally effective, but it was certainly not going to be cheap.

There was nothing for it, but to produce a conventional frame, but at least the company had a great deal of up-to-date knowledge about such components, Until the arrival of the Triumph Mayflower, after all, every Standard car had had a separate frame, and the Triumph TR3, which was still working its way up to full popularity, was also a separate-frame design.

Early in 1957, therefore, with Harry Webster now in charge of the engineering division, a start was made on the mechanical design, the layout of the frame being entrusted entirely to Ralph Wigginton. There was no question, however, of Webster leaving his staff to get on with the car as a team, while he merely pulled a few strings, and administered the project. Everyone who ever worked for Webster (and that includes the author) knows that he was always a 'hands-on' designer, who liked nothing better than to avoid staff meetings, and

The date on this picture is 7 January 1958 – just two weeks after the first Michelotti coupé style arrived in Coventry, from Turin. The car was registered VRW 582, and its shape was not altered, even in detail, before the car went into production

The tail lamps of this prototype, of course, would be altered before production began, but almost every other aspect of the Michelotti-styled 'Zobo' would be retained. Note, however, that the well-known bonnet latches had not then been produced

spend time either sketching out new ideas, or driving test cars that incorporated them.

The styling of the new car, however, was going to provide many headaches, principally because the company had no experienced stylist at this time! Up until the outbreak of the Second World War, all creative styling had been carried out for Standard by suppliers like Pressed Steel, Briggs Motor Bodies, or Fisher & Ludlow. For the first ten years after that war, the company's chief body engineer was Walter Belgrove, who had once been responsible for stylish 1930s Triumphs like the Dolomites. At Standard, he produced the Vanguards Phase I and Phase II, the Triumph TR2, the still-born TRX which preceded it, and the SC 8 hp and 10 hp range.

Belgrove, however, always found it difficult to get on with Ted Grinham, and by the mid-1950s they were barely on speaking terms. The company's decision to award the styling contract for the Series III Vanguard to an American freelance, Carl Otto, hurt him very badly, and it was at the Motor Show of 1955 where that car was exhibited that the final, bitter, row between the two took place. The result was that Belgrove left the company at once (Grinham, after all, *was* deputy managing director . . .), the directors later agreeing that he had been dismissed through no fault of his own—and the company was left without a top stylist.

In 1956–7, therefore, the company had a very capable chief body designer in Arthur Ballard, but he was not, and did not pretend to be, a styling engineer. Mulliners Ltd was still independent of Standard (although they had styled the Renown and Mayflower models, and although they were becoming increasingly beholden to Standard for their future business), and their chief stylist, Leslie Moore, could not spend all his time working for Alick Dick and Harry Webster.

The happy links between Standard, and the dapper little Italian, Giovanni Michelotti, came during the spring and summer of 1957, but before then a number of attempts were made to produce a two-door body style for the new separate chassis car. Artists' renderings of a gradually developing shape have survived in the company's archive, and are reproduced in these pages. The best that I can say of them is that they show a sturdy, but definitely Plain-Jane appearance.

'We had tried and tried with all these styles in Coventry, and what we finished up with was a mechanical bathtub on wheels. I can't describe it as anything else. It looked dreadful!' So said Harry Webster, many years after the event, and John Lloyd more recently reinforced that judgement with the remark that: 'It wasn't just awful, it was *very* awful! We actually built one shell, an open version of that style, and ran it on the very first chassis, that went out to Michelotti.'

Before then, however, chassis design, and mechanical layout, was going on apace. Incidentally, it had been necessary to give the car a project name, for this, and other new designs, were all causing confusion around the place. Webster says that he told one of his administrators to go and find all the names beginning with 'Z'—almost as a joke, at the time—but the manager took his advice, and soon returned with a very impressive list.

Among them was the word 'Zobo', which took Webster's fancy, for reasons which soon became clear. A Zobo is a Tibetan pack animal of indeterminate sex, half-way between a bull and a cow. Believe me, somehow or other that is what the lumpy thing looked like at first!

[There would be other 'Z' names, including Zebu (a humped ox) applied to a new six-cylinder saloon project to replace the Vanguard, Zoic (the six-cylinder Vanguard itself), Zest and Zoom (TR-replacement sports car studies), Zany (the small-engined Atlas van), Zero (the Standard, *not* Ferguson, tractor project), and Zeta (which might have applied to an enlarged Herald, though it was first considered as an entirely new style on the existing 10/Pennant floor pan).]

Then, almost by chance, Webster and Martin Tustin encountered the amazingly talented Michelotti, who had his own independent design and prototype studios in Turin, but who still had strong links with Vignale, who produced bodyshells in some numbers for Supercar concerns like Ferrari and Maserati.

The catalyst was the Flower family, led by Captain Raymond Flower, who approached the company regarding engine and other mechanical supplies for a car (the Frisky) which he was proposing to sell in Egypt. In the course of discussions, Flower admitted that he did not even have a style for his car, but said that that was no problem, as he could get a prototype built in only three months.

'I didn't believe this,' Harry Webster says, 'so we challenged him to get his stylist (who we still didn't know) to produce a body in three months and we would pay for it.'

Flower would not say where this body was to come from, but returned within ten days carrying half a dozen sketches from which a choice was made. A Triumph TR3 rolling chassis was provided, and within three months Flower reappeared with the sensational black-and-white 'dream car', which cost the company only £3000. Only then did the facts emerge—that Giovanni Michelotti had styled the bodyshell, which came complete with tail fins, hooded headlamps and a painted 'spear' along the flanks, and that on this occasion construction was by Vignale in Turin.

Almost immediately, therefore, Michelotti was offered, and accepted, a freelance styling contract with Standard, and soon he had struck up a close, and lasting personal and professional friendship with Webster. In the months and years to come, the engineering director came to know the French and Swiss roads between the English Channel and Turin almost as well as any he normally used in Great Britain. At one stage he went out to Italy every two weeks or so, usually over a weekend so that little time was lost away from the factory.

Michelotti's first job for Standard was to improve the existing Vanguard Series III, and merely by retouching the grille, front and rear lights, wheel discs, and producing a new facia, he made an excellent job of this. Called the 'Vignale Vanguard', this kept the old-fashioned car alive for a while longer, before it could be further rejuvenated by the addition of a six-cylinder engine in 1960. *That* engine, as we shall see, had a real bearing on the career of the separate-chassis cars in the early 1960s.

It was not, on the other hand, easy to do anything about a body style for the Zobo. The only existing car was sent out to Turin during the summer of 1957, and Michelotti tinkered with it for weeks, but as Harry Webster confirms, he was really getting nowhere. By late summer, chassis design was well advanced, and factory planners were looking forward to replacing the old 8 hp and 10 hp models—but with no end to the styling saga in sight, the company's management was getting desperate.

Harry Webster then went off on holiday, with his wife and daughter: 'On the way down I called in on Michelotti in Turin. There was still nothing doing, but I decided to call in on my way back from Sorrento in September.'

The meeting which followed was historic. Parking his car outside, in the Turin city street, Webster went up to the roof-top studio to see what Michelotti had been able to do in two weeks. Nothing! It was hopeless.

'Then I said something like: "We are wasting our bloody time. Look, suppose you could start from scratch, here in Italy, based only on this chassis, what would you propose?" Well, to Michelotti that was like a red rag to a bull.

Michelotti's suggestion for the grille and badge style was thought to be a touch extreme, and too costly to produce. The front panel latches, as seen here, only featured on the first prototype schemes

Within three or four minutes he had sketched-up the Herald as we now know it, and we instantly started transferring this to a full-scale draft on the wall.'

In several interviews about this occasion, Webster has never deviated in any detail, and the events of that day—and evening—are clearly vivid in his memory. It is also certain that he and the Italian stylist became so excited in what was evolving, and so wrapped up in their work, that they completely forgot the passage of time. At around midnight, therefore, when he finally went back to his car, he found his wife and daughter still inside, curled up, fast asleep!

It was a complete breakthrough. Michelotti had started with the car which became the Coupé, and during the night (he worked right through) he also went on to sketch up the other cars in the proposed range. The following day, Webster cabled Alick Dick, back in Coventry, effectively saying 'Hold everything, we've solved the problem', and within 24 hours he was triumphantly driving back towards Coventry with a complete sheaf of one-eighth scale drawings—front, rear, side elevation, and sections—of all the proposed cars.

'I'd also got Michelotti to agree,' Webster says, 'that if I got an immediate go-ahead on the project when I returned to Coventry, then we could have our first prototype shell finished by the end of 1957.'

The promise of a completed shell, not just a mock-up, within three months, was almost too much to hope for, so it was with great joy that the directors greeted the arrival of a truck from Turin, quite literally on the afternoon of Christmas Eve, 1957. Alick Dick and Harry Webster both have the same memories of that day. As Alick Dick recalls:

'We put it straight into the styling studio, on the turntable, and we were all so thrilled with that Coupé body style that we all downed tools and went out for a pint!'

The original 'Zobo' saloon arrived in Coventry in April 1958, and compared with the earlier coupé it had no exterior bonnet latches at all. Like the coupé, its duo-tone colour scheme would be changed before production began

Three-quarter rear view of the very first 'Zobo' saloon prototype, in the styling studio at Coventry, after arrival from Italy. I cannot identify those tail lamp clusters, which are certainly not Standard-Triumph, or even British – most probably an Italian component, already being used on another production car of the day!

Webster is even more emphatic:

'Inside (the truck) was a black and metallic silver coupé . . . Alick Dick and the rest of the board turned up. Everybody thought it was superb. Afterwards we all went down to the canteen and got gloriously drunk!'

All this, of course, is stepping ahead of the evolution of the chassis and its running gear, which had come a long way in recent months. By May 1957, a 'paper chassis design' existed—which is to say that there were designs on paper, but nothing yet complete and running, and the building of the very first frame was about to take place.

The company, in fact, had a very difficult time in settling the layout, not least because they wanted to contain costs on the one hand, but offer an advanced specification on the other. Up until the mid-1950s, the general specification of British economy cars had been depressingly dull, and backward—solid rear axles, leaf spring suspension, and front-engine/rear-drive layouts being the 'norm'. Then, in 1955, the rear-engined, all-independent Fiat 600, inspired by Dott. Dante Giacosa, had arrived, to line up alongside the rear-engined Renault Dauphine of February 1956, and a wave of new thinking swept across Europe. To keep up with the times—or so it seemed to Standard's directors—it was necessary to make a much more advanced car than the ageing Eights and Tens.

The result of this was that the designers decided to specify independent rear suspension, which was still a startling concept for a British car, along with rack-and-pinion steering. To keep costs within bounds, however, it had to be a very simple system, which explains why a transverse leaf spring, and swing axle geometry, was chosen. A more complex system was certainly considered, right from the start, but all other types were rejected, for they would have needed two expensive universal joints.

At the front, however, the first independent suspension design featured a transverse leaf spring (actually inside a main chassis member), and wishbone layout. Once again, this was chosen for cost reasons—one large leaf spring being cheaper than two coils, at that time—and also because it was a layout well-known to the company. The Standard Flying Eight of 1938, and the larger-engined Flying Twelves and Fourteens, all built in Coventry after the end of the Second World War, had all used similar systems, as had the tubular-frame Triumph Roadsters and 1800 saloons introduced in 1946.

The very first car, that with the 'bathtub' style of bodyshell, was tested on the pavé at MIRA with such a leaf-spring suspension, and it was during these tests that it was decided that the front suspension linkage was lacking in stability and precision.

It is also interesting to note that the original design of spring 1957 (the '60 mph/60 mpg' variety) included the 803 cc 'Gold Seal' engine, which produced 33 bhp (gross) at 5000 rpm—perhaps 28 bhp (net)—a cable-operated clutch, a single vacuum-operated wiper blade on the driver's side (the passenger side wiper was to be an optional extra), and it was possible that 4.80-12 in. tyres and wheels might be used instead of the more costly 5.20-13 in. type.

Fortunately for us all, and for Herald/Vitesse/Spitfire/GT6 enthusiasts all round the world, the concept of Zobo as such a very cheap, minimum-specification, model was soon abandoned. For one thing, the end of the Suez/petrol rationing crisis soon restored the buyers' confidence—British car sales boomed up to no less than 1,353,000 a year in 1960—but history also tells us that such stripped-out machines have usually flopped. Consider how this original type of Zobo would have fared, for instance, against the front-wheel-drive sophistication of the BMC Mini, which arrived on the market just four months behind it?

It was during the summer of 1957, therefore, that the definitive Zobo layout began to emerge. There was more than one chassis design, as the pictures in this book confirm, but Wigginton's final layout was much like the first, except in the way that suspension pick-up points, and damper towers, were arranged.

In essence, it was a 'backbone' layout, with three-inch square section box members running parallel with the ground, almost in the centre of the car between the seats, linking the front suspension cross-member to the massive cross-member supporting mountings for the chassis-located final drive, and the rear damper towers. Naturally it was splayed out at the front, to embrace the engine bay, and also at the rear around the final drive, though the single-piece propeller shaft nestled cosily above it: there were depressions in the section under the line of the rear drive shafts, to give them space to articulate.

To complete a chassis platform, ready to support a whole variety of body styles, there were three outriggers at each side—one at the front of the front footwells, one under the line of the front seats, and one at a slight angle under the rear seats—all linked up to channel section outer side members, to which the body sills were to be fixed on assembly of the bodies. Behind the line of the final drive there were two splayed-out box section members, actually extensions of the main backbone members, leading to the extreme corners of the boot floor, and to the bumpers themselves.

At the front, there were box section front members kicking up from the front suspension cross members to the full-width tubular member which supported front underside bodywork, bumpers, and also the pivots for the bonnet/front wings section. Most interesting of all was the provision of bolt-on pressed-steel towers providing pick-up points for the front suspension and dampers.

Having rejected a transverse leaf spring front suspension, the Zobo might still have been equipped with a conventional coil spring and wishbone independent linkage, such as the SC models had had since 1953, if it had not been for an unofficial feet-on-the-table meeting a few of the directors had at Alick Dick's house, at Hill Wootton, near Kenilworth.

As Harry Webster told me: 'Martin Tustin was an extraordinarily quick thinking man, a chap who kept throwing out ideas—occasionally we'd catch one, and it would work.' The idea, on this occasion, was that he said: 'Wouldn't it be marvellous if it (the Zobo) would turn like a London taxi'—which meant that it would need a turning circle of no more than 25 feet.

This was possible, of course, but only by providing a formidable wheel lock, and to do this a new set of links, and a fresh look at the cast vertical link, were needed. The result was a wide-based layout, in which combined coil spring/damper units were used, in which the wheel's back lock was no less than 50 degrees, and in which a light, and very precise, rack-and-pinion steering gear was incorporated. This was the first time rack-and-pinion had ever been used on a Standard model, and the sub-assemblies were all provided by Alford and Alder from Hemel Hempstead.

At the rear, the swing axle independent rear suspension had its transverse leaf spring (eight leaves on home market cars) clamped to the top of the final drive casing under a six stud plate, there were inclined telescopic dampers behind the line of the exposed drive shafts, and—to complete the rear wheel location, fore and

Rear view of the first-ever 'Zobo' saloon prototype, at Standard's styling studio

after—there were tubular radius arms, angled slightly inboard towards the front, linking the vertical links to the chassis frame outriggers.

The most important decision of the period, however, was to abandon any idea of using an 803 cc engine, and to choose the 948 cc engine instead. Not only that, but it was also decided to use two different engine tunes—the more powerful twin-SU engine (effectively a productionized version of the Alexander kit approved for fitment to all the 10 hp SC cars) being reserved for the Coupé and Convertible at first.

This was a very wise move, especially as it transpired that Zobo would be considerably heavier than originally hoped. The thought of an 803 cc engine struggling to provide adequate performance for a 1765 lb car is not reassuring; as it was, the definitive Herald was often criticized for being too slow, too thirsty, and too low geared.

This, however, was only the start. With time already running against Standard, and with body tooling still to be commissioned, there was a great deal still to do.

The interior of the 'Zobo' saloon car prototype of spring 1958. Somehow, over the years, Michelotti's interiors were never as successful as his exterior styles. On this car, the steering wheel and column was unfamiliar (Italian Fiat, almost certainly), while the speedometer/fuel gauge dial was from a Standard Ten of the period

Chapter 3
Turn Left for Tangier: the development period

Because of the indecision over body styling, Zobo's chassis design was always well ahead of body engineering. Once Michelotti's proposals had been agreed, and his workshops had been unleashed to build the first prototype shells, complete cars came together quite quickly.

The car which had electrified the directors on Christmas Eve 1957 was registered VRW 582, carried chassis number X608, and much later found its way to Australia. In the meantime, another coupé, identical in almost every way, took X597, and was registered VRW 589. Early in 1958, it was shipped direct from Turin to Spain, where it was instantly subjected to some fast, dusty, endurance driving to assess the general character of the new design.

Pictures I reproduce show that Les Makinson and Len Knight gave the car a hard time, and that before it came back to the UK for the first time, both Harry Webster and Martin Tustin found time to try it out as well. Study of these pictures shows that the prototype shape produced by Michelotti was not altered at all before production commenced; only the detail of the radiator grille and badging—and, of course, the style of the duo-tone paint scheme—was altered.

ABOVE *VRW 589 pauses in a hard day's testing in Spain, in the warm spring weather of 1958. Note that this prototype already had the famous 'Herald bonnet latches' in place*

LEFT *The very first Herald endurance test took place in Spain, early in 1958, when VRW 589 was shipped direct from Italy, for Les Makinson (left) and Len Knight to drive*

Next along was X611, registered VKV 75, this being the first saloon shell, and it was on this car that a series of handling tests were carried out on the Dunlop skid pan during the autumn of 1958. There was always the problem of cost to be considered (for there was never any likelihood of Zobo meeting its original targets) and at one time the car was tried without a front anti-roll bar (which was expensive!) The result was that the initial understeer was lost, and the transition to final oversteer was that much more sudden. The photographs prove this. . . .

It was at this point in the programme that the idea of offering yet another interim, or stop-gap car came to the surface. In January 1958 it was still hoped that the Zobo coupé would be ready for launch in October 1958 (with the saloon following in April 1959), and to keep up interest in the existing Pennant it was suggested that Zobo-style independent rear suspension should be offered.

Two prototype Pennants—X617 and X618—were fitted up with such a layout, but speedily rejected. As John Lloyd says: 'They were too noisy, extremely noisy. We had to hang the final drive unit on to the unit construction bodyshell, and we couldn't insulate the transmission and road noises. That's what killed it.'

Michelotti's original contract, for £10,000, had covered the design and construction of Zobo saloon, coupé and estate car shells, but for purely practical reasons the estate car programme was allowed to slip back, and the idea of a fourth variety, the convertible came in ahead of it. All the important testing, in fact, was carried out on coupés or saloons, the first of all the convertibles, later registered 4424 HP, not being ready for a styling viewing until February 1959. Even by this time, incidentally, the idea of a van version of the estate car had

already been conceived, though in the autumn of 1959, well before it was authorized for production, it was viewed in the studio with a high-roof, somewhat Hillman Imp-Husky style.

Before the summer of 1958, however, the focus of prototype build turned to Banner Lane, Coventry, Michelotti having completed his prototypes. It is not generally known, however, that he also engineered the bodyshells, and thought through the permutations of bolt-together body sections, removable roofs, and many other details. Arthur Ballard's design team re-designed every panel, with ease of manufacture, and cost control, in mind, but the general layout was not changed.

X619 was the fourth prototype (registered WVC 934, it was a saloon), X624 was originally a saloon registered WRW 404, and X625 was a coupé, registered WRW 405. Those last two cars feature very strongly in an epic publicity and proving run, described later in this chapter.

Even by this stage, the new car's name had not been resolved. Called Zobo by all and sundry for the first two years (it was a habit at Standard-Triumph—even after a model name had been settled, many managers kept using the code name for ages. In the author's days at Fletchamstead North, the Spitfire was 'Bomb' for a couple of years after it had officially been named), it was not to have been a Herald at first.

LEFT *Martin Tustin (left) and Harry Webster (right) had time to assess the Spanish test car, VRW 589, before it returned to Coventry*

LEFT BELOW *At the end of March 1958, VRW 589 was stripped down to its chassis, for inspection after the long tests in Spain. Note that it still had the prototype style of frame pressings at the front, and the big above-axle support pressing at the rear. That is an Atlas van frame in the background*

BELOW *Much handling assessment was carried out on the Dunlop skid pan in Birmingham in September 1958. In this test the saloon is being tried without a front anti-roll bar, and the results are obvious!*

There was little doubt, though, that it was going to be a Triumph, rather than a Standard. The Standard marque had a good, though stodgy, image, and during the 1950s all the good publicity had been gained by the TR2 and TR3 sports cars, which were Triumphs. Many export models were rebadged as Triumphs—the Triumph 10, for example, was a Standard 10 under a new name—and the sales division were no longer in doubt as to the most marketable title.

In some markets, after all, a 'standard' car was the lowest-equipped of a range, while a Triumph was often 'triumphant' in the salesrooms, on race tracks, or in rallies. Although the directors did not make any public announcement for some time, it was generally agreed that the Standard Pennant, the Standard Vanguard Six and the Standard Ensign de Luxe, all being developments of other long-established 'Standard' models, would be the last of the line. The Standard marque did, officially, die in May 1963 as the last of the Ensigns and Vanguards were assembled.

But, for Zobo, Triumph . . . what? A decision seemed to be made in June 1958, when the board of directors 'resolved that the name given to Zobo would be Triumph Torch'. Triumph Torch? Would it have been a winner? Who knows, for it was never to be used.

Certainly there was no broad agreement that 'Torch' was right, and in the end Alick Dick settled the argument, as all managing directors should. One Monday morning he came back to his office, called his colleagues, and said: 'I've been on my boat over the weekend. It's called "Herald". Let's call the new car that.' And so, Herald it was, a name fortunately not already trademarked by any other company, not offensive, or of doubtful meaning, in any other language, and one sufficiently 'different' to

In the autumn of 1958, an ambitious proving exercise, to drive from Cape Town to Tangier, across the Sahara, was tackled. WRW 404 was a Herald saloon, and WRW 405 was a coupé, with a Pennant Companion and an Atlas minibus as service back up. The Heralds were more reliable than the back-up vehicles!

make it clearly identified with this new design.

Meanwhile, the biggest imponderable of all lay with the structure, and assembly, of the bodyshells. The decision to produce the shell in several separate sub-assemblies, then bring them together actually at the assembly stage, had already been taken (as recounted earlier), but the integrity of the designs still had to be checked out.

Taking either the saloon, or the coupé, as my example, I see that the main shell was really split into four large sub-sections, to which the doors and the boot lid were to be fixed. Central to the layout—literally, and actually—was the front footwell/scuttle/windscreen sub-assembly, to which the entire back end/rear wings/boot/rear and centre floor pan section was bolted, by fixings not only going through two metal thicknesses, but also through the central outriggers on the chassis frame. Those outriggers were positioned along the base of the front edges of the front seats.

The third major sub-assembly (though, really, it was little more than one massive pressing) was the roof panel—saloon or coupé as appropriate—which was bolted to the rear deck of the back end of the shell, and to the top of the windscreen, while the fourth was the complete, swing-up, combined bonnet, front wings, nose and inner wheelarches sub-assembly, which hinged at the front of the chassis frame.

To make the car look complete, then, other smaller panels had to be bolted into place—doors and boot lid, of course, along with the pillars behind the door glasses, the sills under the doors and body sides, and the pressings

Simple in-cockpit equipment for the trans-Sahara Heralds – extras including two-way radio, and extra temperature measuring gauges

WRW 404

WRW 405

supporting the grille, and hiding the chassis's built-in bumper bar.

At first there were worries about the sealing between panels, but this never proved to be a problem on new cars, in which appropriate sealing compounds were applied along joints. John Lloyd, whose department carried out the tests, remembers very clearly that the main problem was not to seal the inside of the car from water and dust (and draughts!), but to get rid of creaks, rattles and groans:

'We never realized how good the body *could* be until we actually welded one up, rather like a complete shell, then rubber mounted it to the chassis frame. The torsional rigidity of that welded-up shell was much higher, too.

'We never had any sealing problems around the floor—though we had some trouble stopping water leaks around the screen and the roof. Of course there were problems in sealing the door glasses, which didn't have any frames. We had a look at that, once or twice, later on.'

By the summer of 1958, the plot was taking shape rapidly. The press tools for the different body sections were all being made as fast as possible, plans were being laid for a vast new assembly hall, located alongside existing buildings at Canley, and the takeover of Mulliners (and, therefore, Forward Radiator) was almost complete. Volume assembly—coupés first, and saloons a few weeks later—would begin in February 1959, with the public launch planned for April.

LEFT *John Coquillon, later even more famous as a film cameraman, made an excellent documentary about the Cape Town–Tangier proving run. This, by the way, was a good quality bridge over the African river in question!*

LEFT BELOW *Time for re-fuelling in Africa, with John Lloyd (right) directing operations*

BELOW *John Coquillon capturing the Herald Coupé (and audience) at rest part way across Africa in the autumn of 1958*

Mobilgas
Mobil Diesel
G·B WRW 405

PT.2
TOMBOUCTOU
TESSALIT
G·B WRW 405

For the time being, at least, the obsolescent 8s, 10s and Pennants would continue to be built, though it was thought that home market demand would dry up later in the year. The full Herald range—then planned to include a van and a pick-up, though the pick-up was never put on sale—was all to be available by the spring of 1960.

The Herald, however, was no ordinary new car, and was very special to Standard's future. For that reason, therefore, the company wanted to give it a good send-off, with lots of publicity.

'I don't know how it happened, but Harry and Martin Tustin had clearly been discussing this, maybe with Alick Dick.' John Lloyd still recalls the moment, more than a quarter of a century later:

'One day when I was with prototype cars, testing at MIRA, Web and Tustin arrived, took me on one side said: "How would you like to take a couple of these cars out to Africa and back?"

'Apparently they worked up an idea to ship the cars out to Dakar, drive them down to the Cape, then back to England! I went back home that night, worked out the mileage, realized it was going to be in excess of 20,000 miles, and had to go back to Web and say; "Did you realize how far this is going to be? It isn't on, we'd be away for six months."'

But that was the start of the mad-cap scheme to drive cars all the way across the continent, from Cape Town to London. Not for experimental purposes, you understand (it was far too late for changes to be made to the specification, unless there were catastrophic failures), but to prove out the design, and to gain publicity for the new models.

Starting from Cape Town on 18 October 1958, a small convoy of cars, John Lloyd, cameraman Johnny Coquillon and six fitters from the experimental workshops, finally arrived on the Mediterranean in mid-December, and made it back to the UK before the end of the year.

It was an epic, hazardous, trip, fortunately recorded for posterity, not only by Coquillon's camera, but by journalist Richard Bensted-Smith (then of *The Motor*), who joined the convoy at Kano, accompanied by explorer David Pratt. Not only was a splendid film prepared in time for the world's press to see it at the Herald's launch at the Albert Hall, in London, but Bensted-Smith's story was serialized in *The Motor* in April and May 1959, and later published as a book, thoughtfully titled *Turn Left for Tangier*.

ABOVE LEFT *This refuelling stop, on the legendary Turn Left for Tangier proving run shows that the two prototypes were both in exact 'production specification' except for the discreet lack of badges. The saloon had left-hand drive, but by the time* The Motor *tried it in the spring of 1959 it had been converted to right-hand drive!*

LEFT *There will be no jokes about going to Timbuktu, if you don't mind! In any case, after this lunch halt the cars then made off across the Sahara towards Tessalit*

Only the foolish would have attempted to complete 9650 miles from Cape Town to Tangier—via Elizabethville, Stanleyville, Kano and the Sahara desert—without support, which explains why two prototype Heralds—WRW 404 (chassis number X624) being a saloon, and WRW 405 (chassis number X625) being a coupé—were accompanied by a 948 cc Atlas minibus (coded 'Zany', and carrying registration WRW 403, which made it all very tidy, and easy to remember), and a Standard Pennant Companion (X626, WRW 819).

'It was much more of an adventure than I'd bargained for,' says John Lloyd, who led the expedition. 'We didn't come near to losing anyone, but we certainly encountered circumstances that a group of engineers from Coventry were not even geared up to meet. Medical problems developed, heat exhaustion, a touch of malaria, and so on. Fundamentally the cars weren't ideal either—the Heralds were so heavily laden that they only had a three inch ground clearance, for instance!'

According to John, the basic problem, throughout, was one of time, not keeping the cars going. The trip simply had to be finished by the end of 1958, so that Johnny Coquillon could get the publicity film ready, but the delays caused by bureaucracy, customs posts, visa difficulties, and even the need to avoid terrorist activity in Algeria, all mounted up.

'Yes, road conditions were very difficult at times—we got stuck in the sands 169 times as I recall, but one car always seemed to get through, and tow the others out—though my biggest problem was not with the cars, but in keeping the crew motivated for so long. None of us had *ever* tackled anything like this before!

Naturally there were problems, with all the cars, but the diplomatic Bensted-Smith made light of these in his book. All of them were overloaded, all of the time, and the roads were awful, even where they qualified as roads at all. John Lloyd's letters, air-mailed back to Coventry while the journey was still going on, tell their own story:

'MITWABA, October 31: If you can visualize the Lindley research establishment's corrugated track rolled into the pavé track and dust tunnel, with the cross-country track thrown in for good measure, you have the lot. . . .'

But, later:

'FORT ARCHAMBAULT, November 16: . . . Whatever I've said about bad roads up to now, forget. Today's run has set up completely new standards. . . .'

The Atlas bus suffered more than the cars, for it proved to be undercooled, and the only way to stop it boiling, in blazing temperatures, was to have the heater full on, the whole time. The Pennant Companion, too, was rolled into the bush at least once, and eventually the whole of the front end sheet metal began to part company with the main cabin.

The Herald coped valiantly, at least as far as the chassis, and the bodies were concerned, though eventually they objected to the heavy overload carried right across Africa; they even had piled-high roof racks across the Sahara desert.

'The Heralds gave little trouble,' John Lloyd says, 'except that the front suspensions slowly collapsed. The top wishbone mounting turrets settled, which caused loss of camber, and of ground clearance. We also broke wishbone lower mounts—where they went straight through the chassis rails they eventually snapped off due to embrittlement and fatigue.'

There was also more than one half shaft failure, and after the rear suspension radius rods had contacted the bodyshell on full bump on several occasions, and snapped, the design was hastily changed on all cars. At one time the African team found a tubular flag pole (carried for marking purposes in the desert) very useful for sleeving the breaks!

The problem, after the team had been joined by Bensted-Smith and Pratt, in a Vanguard

RIGHT ABOVE *Across the Sahara desert in November 1958, there was no problem about driving on the left . . . . or the right, for that matter!*

RIGHT *Nearly there now! John Lloyd leaning against the hard-pressed Atlas, with the Herald Coupé and the saloon (both down by the nose due to collapsing suspension towers), Dick Bensted-Smith's Vanguard estate car, and the battered Pennant Companion, lined up after it.* Everyone *was glad to get home*

WRW 403
WRW 404

Estate car, was not to keep the cars and support vehicles going, but to find enough space for all the gear. In the end, John Lloyd decided to ship all but a bare minimum of spares back to Coventry, by sea, from Nigeria, and fill every cranny with fluids:

'We needed a gallon of water, per person, per day, the experts said, so as there were ten of us, and we knew we would be in the desert for ten days, that was a hundred gallons of water. Then we had to carry a lot of spare fuel—we carried a hundred gallons of that, too. Work it out, that's nearly half a ton of each!'

When *The Motor* published Bensted-Smith's features, they subtitled the story 'The Hard Way for Heralds'. It was certainly that, but it was certainly a sensational way to bring the new car to the attention of the public. If ever you get a chance to see the film, titled *A New Experience in Motoring*, don't miss it. Incidentally, the Heralds which flogged across the desert were not brand new before they moved out of Cape Town. Far from it—the Coupé had already completed 2000 miles on the MIRA proving ground pavé at Lindley (which is enough for one car's life-time, I can tell you), before being launched into the unknown.

It is only fair to admit that, well before the end of the trans-African marathon, everyone in the team wondered whether it had been worth it. 'We sometimes wondered what we were trying to prove,' John Lloyd now says.

What was certainly proved, make no mistake about this, was that the basic design was sound, and that the cars were ready to go on sale with no more than minor modifications to things like suspension mountings and fixings, axle shafts, and radiator sizes. But once the team stopped in Tangier, and looked across the narrow stretch of water to Gibraltar, they couldn't wait to get home. Tired as they were, they landed in Gibraltar, pointed northwards, and reached England after 46 hours of continuous driving.

The time for testing was now over, and most of the development had been completed. Now it was time for the new car to be launched. What would the public think? Would they queue up to buy the new models? The company was about to find out.

LEFT *Fred Nicklin, posing here for a chewing-gum advert, did much of the test-driving on the Heralds. This is an early example of the convertible*

LEFT BELOW *The definitive chassis, in twin-carb engine form, finally ready to go into production – photographed in the summer of 1958. Don't the wheels look narrow by modern standards!*

BELOW *The first proposal for a Herald van, dating from September 1959. The raised roof line would have been very practical, but expensive to tool-up. Note the fuel tank, still in the saloon car position*

Chapter 4
The Herald on sale: a fight for credibility

When the Triumph Herald was finally put on sale on 22 April 1959, it created a real stir. It was the most excitingly new product to be unveiled by Standard for many years, and it broke just about every existing mass-production rule in the book. The motoring press, who were having a very busy time indeed with new models, were really very kind about the new car.

Perhaps, for the sake of the Herald's impact, it was as well that it was so unconventional. So many interesting new cars were revealed in 1959, in Great Britain, and all round the world, that a conventional car would simply have sunk without trace.

Let me remind the reader that in 1959, the Herald had to compete for headlines with cars as different as the Ford Anglia 105E and the Rolls-Royce Phantom V, the BMC Mini and the Daimler SP250 sports car, the mass of BMC 'Farina' saloons and the Sunbeam Alpine, along with many other facelifted, or freshened up, models.

For the media, the attraction of the Herald was in its layout and construction, rather than its styling. Company publicists had carefully hidden the real reason behind the choice of a separate chassis frame. *The Autocar*, for instance, were encouraged to say that: 'Prolonged study by Standard engineers indicated that the separate chassis frame permits a more rigid structure . . .' (which is rather like gripping one's principles firmly in both hands, and telling the world that Black is really White . . .), while *The Motor* stated that: '. . . a number of suppliers could be called upon for individual pressings, so that the company would not be dependent on a single concern for the supply of complete bodies. . . . The first point that was decided was that a separate chassis was essential and that the body would be built up from easily attached sub-assemblies bolted, rather than welded, together . . .' The truth, they say, is relative, and in this case there was no doubt that a good, solid, virtue had been made out of stark necessity.

Forgetting the controversy of the 'Meccano' construction, however, there was still a lot to interest the media, and of course the public. First, and very important, was the styling, sleek, sharp edged, and utterly different from anything previously seen from Standard. Michelotti's contribution to the Vignale Vanguard, shown at the previous Motor Show, had not been over-played, so this, the first fruit of a very successful relationship, was much more important.

Next there was the use of independent rear suspension, at a time when no other small British family car had such a feature. The fact that it was a swing-axle installation caused no great comment at this time, except that it was clearly a very cost-effective way of providing independence. Fleet Street loved the idea of the tiny turning circle, fit to beat the legendary London taxicab, though it wouldn't be long before the rubber-wearing, tyre-scrubbing, effect of using all that available lock would become clear.

There were several other advanced features. One was the complete absence of grease nipples in the chassis, for according to the launch

Technical chief Harry Webster, 'father of the Herald', sitting on a Herald Coupé's rolling chassis, in 1959, in its original-condition design state

literature no lubrication service was required (apart from regular attention to engine and transmission oil levels) at intervals of less than 10,000 miles. In the front suspension, by Alford & Alder, this was done by providing rubber wishbone bushes for the inner joints, and nylon for the outer joints, a nylon cup for the vertical links upper ball joint, and aluminium-bronze threaded bushes for the lower trunnions (which were provided with built-in oil reservoirs). At the rear end, too, the radius arms had rubber bushes at front and rear pivot points.

Then, of course, there was the adjustable joint in the steering column, which not only allowed the steering column to be moved towards, or away from, the driver, but was supposed to collapse under heavy impact loads, to stop the wheel spearing back into the driver's chest during a head-on accident.

This worked well, but only up to a point. Many crashed Heralds still suffered from columns bent upwards towards the roof, as well as partially protected from the impact. By modern standards the friction plates and clamping nuts would be considered crude, but at a time when no other small British car had such a fitting this was a real advance.

The cars also had much interest to offer, in terms of trim, fittings, and furnishings. To lift forward the bonnet, one was offered nothing less than a sturdy handle, styled into the bonnet centre (how many 'safety' regulations would it fail today?), and on the extreme rear edges of the wings there were the crossed 'Vignale' flags, which apparently had a quite inappropriate nautical meaning.

The facia style, and equipment, was so plain that it caused comment, particularly as the pressed fibreboard used for the panel itself did not look particularly nice. Perhaps the glove box should not have been finished in a contrasting colour on the Coupé (the saloon did not even have one, at this stage), and maybe the

The Herald's production design of differential case support featured a front mount in the form of a pressing, bolted to the case behind the propshaft flange, and to brackets on the chassis backbone members

The first few production Herald bodies were built very cautiously, to check that everything fitted as it should . . .

drop-down oddments tray under the cubby box should not have looked quite so much like a 'chip basket', but it was still a very useful layout. The oddments tray on the tunnel, ahead of the gear lever, was useful, and the driving position was good by any standards.

Little things like the fuel reserve feature (you had to swivel the pick-up pipe on the tank, in the boot, from one position to another, to use the last few pints), the way the rear seat squab on the cars could be let down, giving access to the boot for really bulky objects to be carried, and the provision of a fresh air heater, and screen washers as standard, were all welcome.

Not only were the cars very attractive to look at, but there was also an intriguing new range of colours, including (to the author), the so evocatively named 'Wistaria', and 'Alpine Mauve', and the very trendy (and, for the time, advanced) availability of a Coupé body style.

The problem, however, is that the cars were undeniably expensive. By the time all the extra equipment had been specified (such as the heater and other 'extras') the cars had missed their original targets by quite a lot. When they were put on sale, in April 1959, the Herald saloon was priced at £702, and the Coupé at £731; even then, the rear seat of the Coupé, called 'occasional', and so it was, cost £14 more.

Compare these prices, then, with the Herald's obvious competition: Austin A40 Farina from £639, Ford Anglia 100E from £539, Morris Minor 1000 from £590. For around £710, indeed, one could purchase a Hillman Minx Special, a Vauxhall Victor (well, some did . . .) or even a Morgan 4/4.

In the market place, therefore, the new Herald was going to have to justify its high price by technical excellence, and by high quality standards—quality, not only of materials and fittings, but quality of assembly and inspection. Because of its price, the Herald was much further 'up-market' than the SC model family it would shortly displace, and the customers expected more from it. This, as it turned out, was the Herald's biggest problem, right from the start. The battle, in marketing terms, was for credibility.

That comforting virtue, hindsight, now tells us that the Herald of 1959 had two failings, technically, to add to the problems of quality. Its roadholding, at the limit, was suspect, and it was underpowered. To get the most out of the 948 cc engines—which produced 34.5 bhp (net) in single-carb form for the saloons, and a more spirited 45 bhp (net) in twin-SU form for the Coupé—the gearing had to be low. For the Coupé, 14.2 mph/1000 rpm in top gear was

ABOVE . . . *though this particular shell was one of the first hand-built shells produced at Coventry in the spring of 1958. Note the swaging differences around the propeller shaft tunnel, and the panels above the rear suspension*

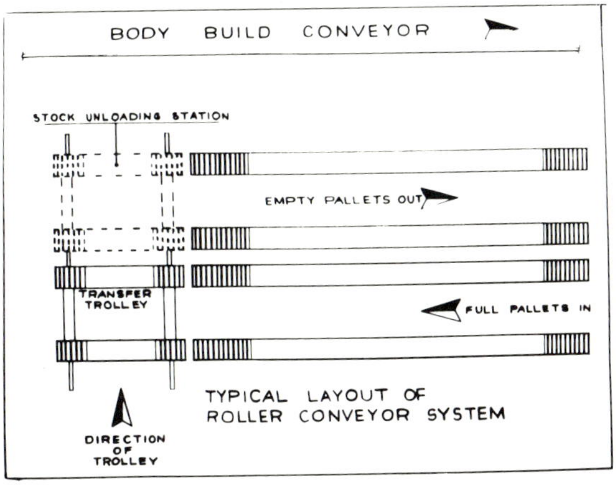

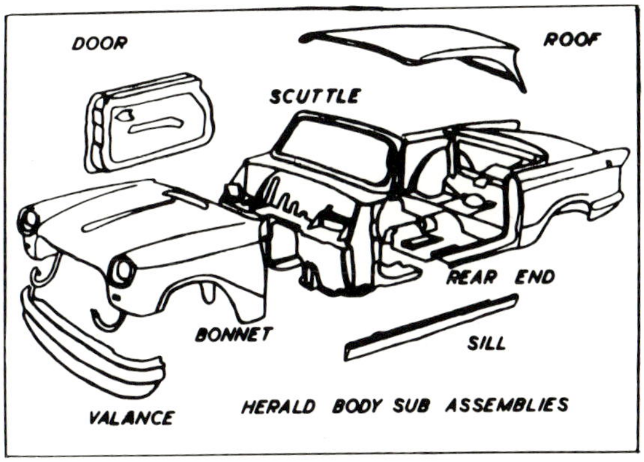

bad enough, but for the saloon it was a miserable 13.2 mph/1000 rpm. This meant, for instance, that to cruise the saloon at 70 mph, the engine was turning over at 5200 rpm, which was well over the power peak.

Yet the motoring press were very kind to the cars at first. *The Autocar*, testing a Coupé, suggested that 'There seems every prospect that the Triumph Herald will have a profoundly good influence on this country's reputation and success in world markets. At home in Great Britain, its special handling qualities will interest and please drivers who pride themselves on their abilities at the wheel. More important, it is a car which flatters an inexperienced or inexpert motorist, and should therefore contribute towards raising present-day standards of road safety.'

Remarkably, in view of what later became known, *The Autocar* wrote: 'The safe high-speed cornering capabilities bring it closer into line with sports-racing practice, and beyond the experience of most everyday drivers. . . . When the car is pressed beyond the limit of tyre

RIGHT COLUMN *These sketches show how the Herald bodyshell was built in sections at Liverpool (Hall Engineering), Wellington (Sankey), Birmingham (Mulliners) and Swindon (Pressed Steel Co.) before being shipped to Coventry for completion*

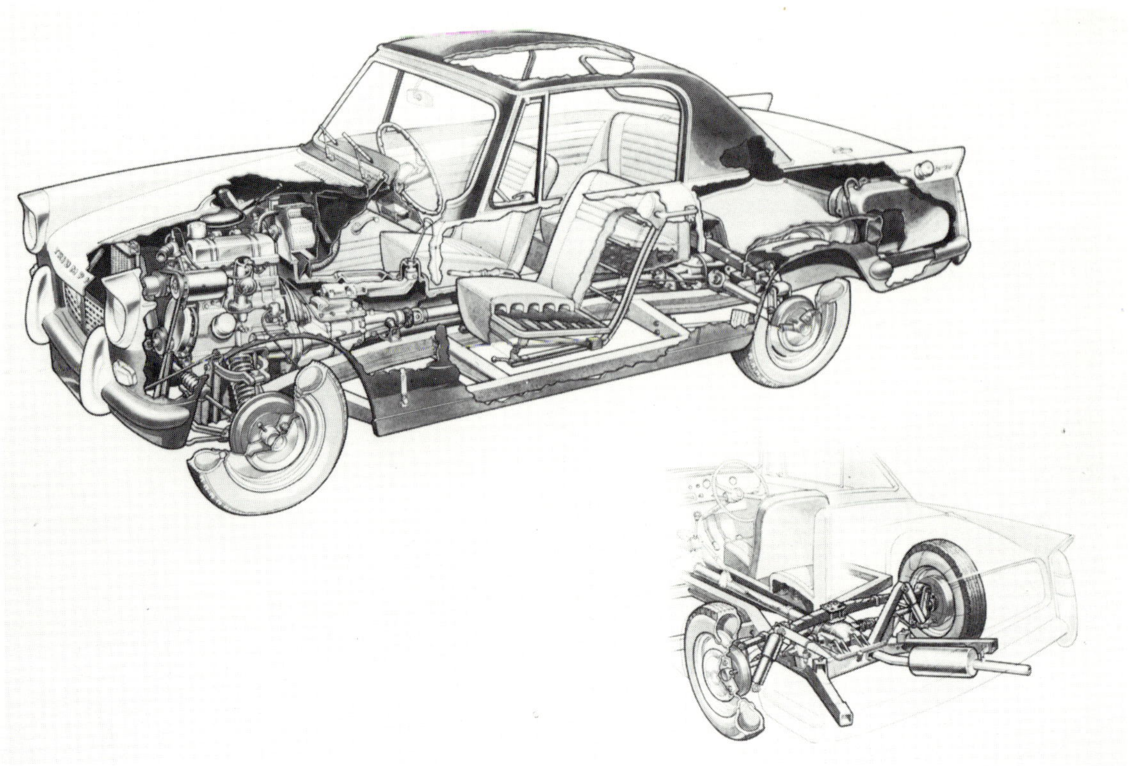

Standard-Triumph's own cutaway drawing of the Herald Coupé, the inset showing detail of the rear suspension

adhesion, the tail end tends to slide first, but the car's habits are predictable and free from peculiarities. On a wet surface, too, the new Triumph behaves extremely well, and has a high degree of wheel grip.'

Remarkable. Could this have been a specially-modified car, with lowered suspension? Apparently not. Not only did *The Motor* have much the same thing to say about their saloon, but this car was no less than WRW 404, the red-and-white car which had featured so dramatically in the Cape Town-to-Tangier escapade at the end of 1958!

That this was not just a case of numberplate swapping is proved by comments elsewhere in the magazine's pages, though it is certain that many 'trans-African' components would have been ditched, and replaced by new items. In this test, however, it was interesting that the ever-diplomatic *Motor* had their own ideas about gearing, stating that: '. . . 60 mph is, perhaps, the best cruising speed of all, with the willing engine, the low level of wind noise and the good suspension combining to give the impression of a much larger car. So, too, does the unusual top-gear flexibility.'

So much, of course, might have been expected of Britain's two 'establishment' weeklies, but when *Motor Sport*, whose editor Bill Boddy could be quite unreasonably waspish when the mood took him, said the same things, one had to sit up and take notice.

Motor Sport's test car was a Coupé, the five-page analysis was headlined 'Britain's Outstanding New Car', and comment included these pearls:

'The verdict? That this new Triumph . . . a car notable for . . . outstanding road-holding, steering, and cornering, is way out ahead of all other small cars at present being made in this country.'

Which was all well and good, but Boddy was surprisingly relaxed about a whole series of failures which occurred on the car during his tenure. The roof lining became detached (and

Sideways assembly in the old assembly hall, according to tradition, in February 1959, when every one of the first cars was a coupé. Most of these cars have right-hand drive. Why does that nearest the camera have taped-up badges?

pressed down on the driver's head at speed—very novel!), the driver's door pull came loose, passenger seat support hinges didn't work properly, a silencer weld came adrift, a front carpet rucked back, and the edge of one door pocket chafed away. It was *that* sort of failing which was going to give the Herald such a hard time in the months, and years, which followed.

The problem was that preparations for building the car at a rate of 2000 cars a week had had to be completed at a furious rate. Hall Engineering Ltd, through their subsidiary Auto Body Dies, had not started cutting body press tools until 7 January 1958, but finished the job on 19 February 1959.

The big rush had not only been to get bodyshell tooling complete, but to finalize sources of supply for the major sections. The biggest 'piece of Meccano', the rear end, was produced by Forward Radiator/Mulliners, Pressed Steel Co. actually supplied roofs, Hall Engineering and Sankeys were also involved. It was Sankey, too, who got the job of producing the chassis frames.

While all this was going on, Alick Dick and the Standard Motor Co. Ltd board were heavily involved in huge financial manoeuvres, bids, counter-bids, and battles. Since this is all germane to the Herald's career, I ought to describe the events of 1957 to 1960 at this point:

Immediately after the Second World War, Sir John Black had concluded a historic agreement with Harry Ferguson, whereby Standard would assemble Ferguson tractors at Banner Lane. This did remarkable things for Standard's profits and cash-flow over the years.

In 1953, however, Ferguson sold his business to Massey-Harris of Canada, and thereafter relations between M-H-F and Standard began to deteriorate. Nevertheless, with Alick Dick always on the look-out for a larger concern with which he could merge, talks about an amalgamation were held in 1957, but these

soon developed into a bid for control from M-H-F, which Dick rejected. The tractor concern, having been rebuffed, were furious, and tried to gain control by buying up the balance of Mulliners business when Standard agreed to absorb it in the summer of 1958.

That was the final straw for Dick and his board, who set about cutting themselves free from the tractor-building business completely. Dick, it seems, decided to sell out, for cash, and to use that cash to buy up other companies, or facilities, and to enlarge the Canley site. The unscrambling process began in the spring of 1959, just after the Herald had been revealed, and was complete in the summer of that year. It meant that the Standard top management would have to move out of Banner Lane, into the Canley site, and that the entire design, development and testing facility would have to leave Banner Lane; fortunately there was a self-contained building adjacent to the Coventry-pass, known as the Fletchamstead North site, to which Harry Webster's department moved at the end of 1959.

In the meantime, the company had moved into the ex-Ministry of Supply factory at Radford, to build Herald transmissions and final drives there, had begun to rationalize the Beans Industries foundries at Tipton, Staffs and had smoothly absorbed the Mulliners operations in Birmingham.

In 1958, however, there were two other important developments in Coventry, one a new building project, the other the result of rather fortuitous purchase. The new building was the huge new assembly hall at Canley (which, by 1961, would allow the old facility to be cleared, and put to new use), and the purchase was of the old Fisher & Ludlow factory at Tile Hill!

BOTH LEFT *Two views of the Herald Coupé cutaway car which Standard-Triumph produced for inspection when the new car was launched in 1959. The backrest angle of the rear seat, and the headroom provided, could hardly be described as comfortable. There's no space wasted, though, especially around the contours of the transmission*

For Alick Dick, at this point, revenge (over BMC) must have been very sweet, for it was Sir Leonard Lord's refusal to provide Fisher & Ludlow facilities for the Zobo project which had led to the entire separate-chassis/sectioned-body concept in the first place.

Who knows what plans BMC might once have had for the Tile Hill factory at one time? The fact was, though, that during 1958 it became clear that the Standard 8/10/Pennant business would soon begin to fall away, and that F & L did not want to bring any new assembly into the building.

Alick Dick, therefore, had talks with Sir George Harriman (BMC's chairman), established that the Tile Hill plant, which was only two miles away from Canley, would be of no further use to BMC, and agreed to buy it. The deal was done by November 1958, and was officially announced in the week that the Herald was put on sale. Tile Hill would become Standard property in November 1959, and from the beginning of 1960 it would be ready for use as a paint and trim plant for the Heralds. An operational nicety was that it would actually become a 'Mulliners' factory, controlled by Mulliners' management.

The building of the new assembly hall at Canley, however, was an even bigger project. There was undeveloped land to the west of the much-enlarged original Canley site (it had originally been built in 1916, for aeroplane assembly, incidentally!) and Standard wanted to use this to make many more cars than ever before. Helped along by this new three-storey hall, it was at one time planned to build up to 160,000 cars a year, of which 100,000 would be Heralds, 30,000 would be large saloons, and 21,000 would be TR sports cars. To make so many Heralds—25 cars an hour—would need double-shift working. Capital expenditure of £2 million for this was sanctioned in October 1958.

The new facility, however, would not be ready for use until the end of 1960, and until then the production of Heralds was going to be a less-than-ideal business, even though yet another body pressings business (Hall Engineering) was purchased at the end of 1959, at

LEFT *A show finished example of the 948 cc Herald Coupé's engine/gearbox assembly, as launched in 1959 . . .*

LEFT BELOW . . . *though this was the more usual standard of finish! Thinks – four fan blades on the show engine, but only two blades on this example*

RIGHT *The Herald engine's camshaft was on the left of the cylinder block, with drive to it by chain. All the main electrical components – starter motor, dynamo, distributor and spark plugs, were also on the left side*

BELOW *The original 948 cc Herald's gearbox had an integrally cast clutch bell housing, all in light alloy, but this was changed, in the interests of sound deadening and rigidity, during the life of the car. The same remote control extension was also to be used in the very successful Spitfire of 1962*

ABOVE *The original single-carb Herald saloon engine bay of 1959, with a wheel and mounted side curtain protection, from mud thrown up by the wheels*

RIGHT ABOVE *The Herald had a remarkable 25 foot turning circle, which was only possible because the wheels could be turned so far – like this. It made great headlines, but the tyre scrub penalty was serious*

RIGHT *The simple facia/instrument panel layout of the twin-carb. Heralds, various – left to right, fuel gauge, speedometer and engine water temperature gauge*

the same time as the Alford & Alder suspensions and steering gear specialists were also annexed.

There had been important corporate changes in the same period. The name 'Triumph' did not appear in the main holding company's title until 1959, though a sales operation, known as Standard-Triumph International, had been set up in January 1958. To reflect the imminent split with Massey-Harris-Ferguson, the company's car business was hived off and titled Standard Motor Co. (1959) Ltd, and a tractor 'shell' company was to be called the Standard Tractor Co. (1959) Ltd. Then came the final divorce from M-H-F. To reflect this, and to reflect the growing importance of the Triumph marque, the main company became Standard-Triumph International Ltd from September 1959, and it was this concern which would be taken over by Leyland less than two years later.

In the meantime, Herald assembly struggled to get established, not only because of the geographically-separated sources of supply, but because of bottlenecks in paint, trim and assembly that would only be solved by the opening up of Tile Hill, and the new assembly hall at Canley. A measure of the problem is that

TRIUMPH
XHP 245

in the whole of 1959, only 4227 Herald Coupés, and 22,404 Herald saloons were produced—a figure which would comfortably be doubled in 1960, even though the market itself had turned down.

By mid-summer 1959, though, the first two Herald types were becoming established, the UK market as a whole was booming ahead, and the 'You've Never Had It So Good' general election would follow in November. Standard-Triumph, therefore, pressed ahead with all the Herald developments in the pipe-line.

Next to appear was what is now known as the 'Twin Carb saloon'—quite simply, the Herald saloon, with the 45 bhp engine, and transmission ratios, of the coupé. The basic price went up by £25, the total price from £702 to £737—and, this, incidentally, made the twin-carb saloon £6 more costly than the coupé.

With export markets in mind, however—and to help align the Herald to the TR3A, which also carried the 'Triumph' badge—the important addition to the range was the new Convertible, which made its debut in March 1960. The car shown to the press—XKV 864—carried chassis number X641, and was the very first Coventry-built experimental machine. It was a very smart machine, based closely on the rear body decking of the coupé, rather the saloon, and had a fully-concealed hood, when this was retracted.

The convertible, too, was fitted with the coupé's engine and drive line, and was an 'almost four-seater'. The price, on announcement, was a total of £766, which made it the most expensive Herald so far, and among the optional extras was a full-length tonneau cover, with a zip fastener down the middle, for £11.33.

The problem, though, was that by this time the Herald's reputation was already on the

LEFT *The Herald boot compartment, minus floor covering, showing the spare wheel position, the seven gallon fuel tank, and the simple bracing of the boot lid itself*

LEFT BELOW *The original Herald was available either with duo-tone paintwork . . .*

BELOW *. . . or as a single-colour scheme. On balance, the duo-tone looked best, and was very popular*

skids. It was not merely that it was expensive, and not merely that there were important (and successful) rival new models in the Ford Anglia 105E and the BMC Mini-Minor. It was, quite literally, that too many early Heralds were falling to pieces on their new owners. The car's quality was not up to scratch, the word got around, and sales began to fall away. The quality problem was also compounded by the difficulty in keeping the built-up bodies water-tight.

RIGHT *Was the original coupé roof style too plain? Triumph stylists thought so, and produced this attractive ribbed rear quarter, which was introduced in mid-1960. It was no coincidence that it made the roof easier to produce, and that there was also a rain gutter above the ribbing*

RIGHT BELOW *Although the frame used in this shot is actually that of a Spitfire, the detail of the Herald's independent front suspension, combined spring/damper units, and rack and pinion steering are all ideally displayed. Drum brakes on a Spitfire, along with a single carb. engine? Don't worry – that was an installation check only, on the prototype Spitfire*

BELOW *The coupé had a most attractive roof line, hiding what were, in fairness, only '+2' rear seats*

Early in 1960, everything started to go wrong for Standard-Triumph, and for the Herald. Sales forecasts, circulated in February, suggested that 136,000 Heralds could be sold in 1960–1961, with 158,500 a year later, and no fewer than 175,000 the year after that. This, in the event, was ludicrously over-optimistic. In 1960–1961, in fact, only about 70,000 Heralds were built, and the figure would fall yet again in 1961–1962.

Then the situation was made worse when the 1960 Budget brought a tightening of the domestic credit squeeze, and when a recession all round the world began to bite. The sales department raised the alarm for the first time in April 1960 (just after the Herald Convertible had been launched), and repeated that warning in July. It was in the summer of 1960 that Herald production was trimmed back for the first time, and in September it was cut back again.

Profits (which had been £1.8 million for the year ending 31 August 1960), suddenly turned into big losses, and in Alick Dick's own words:

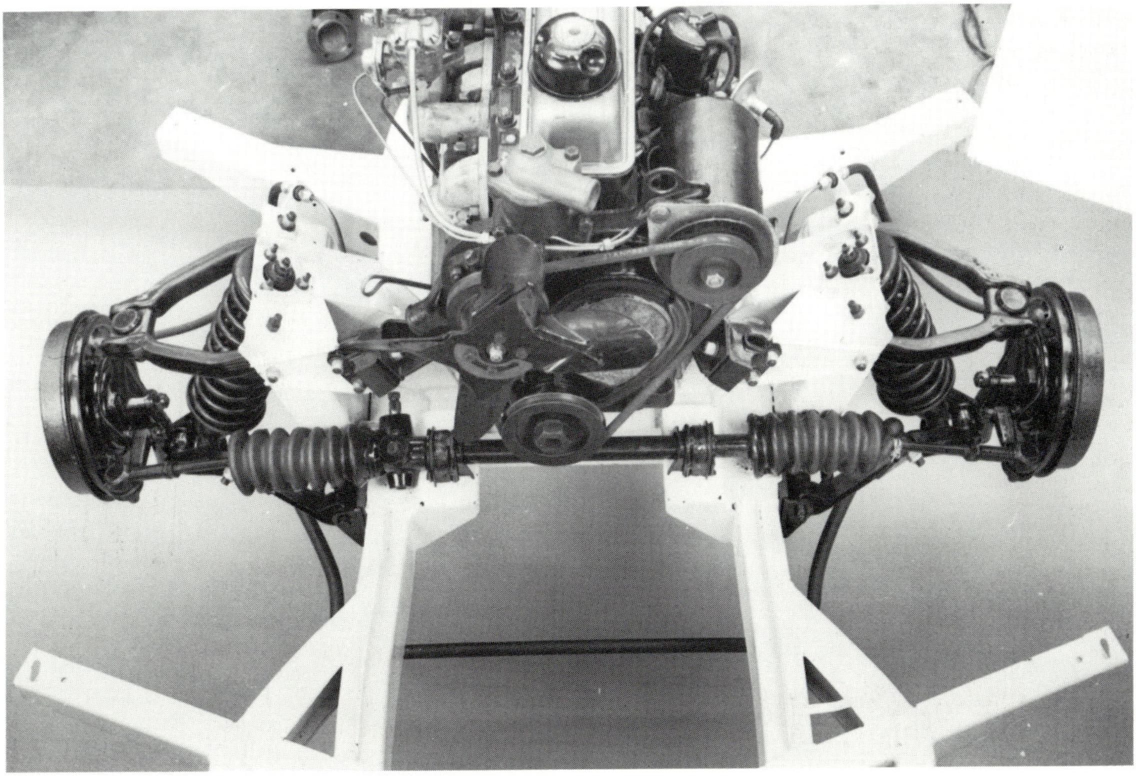

XKV 864

XKV 864

'Money poured out of the company like water. It was absolutely terrifying. We moved from £6 million in the black to £4 million in the red.'

The first takeover approaches from Leyland Motors, which were made in November 1960, came at exactly the right time, but it was not until the spring of 1961 that they were formalized. In the meantime, Standard-Triumph made one further attempt to liven up sales of 948 cc Heralds until the 1200 version was ready.

The quality problem, it was reasoned, could be solved, and *was* being solved, but the pricing problem was serious. It was difficult to convince a customer, in the showroom, that the Herald was really much better equipped than its rivals, for their placarded costs *without* extras like heaters, were what attracted attention in the first place.

Accordingly, like so many other car-makers before, or since, the company decided to produce a stripped-out model, at a rock-bottom price. Perhaps it was not to be a 'loss-leader', in supermarket terms, but it was meant to have the same effect.

The new derivative, sold only as a saloon, was to be called Herald S, and was a starkly equipped machine by any standards. The 'S' was never explained, but my friends on *The Autocar* decided that it meant 'S for Simplicity', and headlined their description in those terms.

Compared with the original Herald saloon, the S had most of its exterior brightwork missing, there was no central bonnet-lifting handle, and the grille was simple mesh without the decoration. Inside the car, a heater was not normally fitted, neither was the screen washer, and there were rubber mats, rather than carpets, in the front footwells. Duo-tone paintwork was not available, though surprisingly enough the twin-carburettor kit (for £21.25) still was.

LEFT ABOVE *Third of the Herald derivatives to go on sale was the Convertible, which had a twin-carb, Coupé-specification. engine. It looked equally smart with the hood erect . . .*

LEFT . . . *or with it folded completely away*

ABOVE *Convertible assembly, mixed in with coupés and saloons. This was the joy of the Herald, that all assembly processes were so flexible*

TOP *The foldaway Herald convertible hood, half way up (or down!)*

CENTRE *The convertible opened up, not only showing off the neat stowed-away hood condition, but the general layout of the facia of all cars fitted with the twin-carb. engine*

ABOVE *The Herald S's facia was even more plain than that of other Heralds, with no glove box lid, and no 'chip basket' underneath*

TOP *'Bargain basement' model – the down-market Herald S, launched in February 1961, with a very plain grille, and badging for identification*

RIGHT *Some time later, the four-door style was sold to the Standard Motor Products of India subsidiary, and eventually became the Standard Gazel, complete with modified 13/60 style bonnet and frontal appearance*

The price, the all-important new 'feature' was down to £664, compared with the £702 of the original saloon—a saving of only £38, but one which the sales force, and the dealer showrooms, could make some noise about. Not, of course, that it was going to help much, because the Herald S was still more expensive than the Anglia 105E (£589 upwards, depending on equipment), or the BMC Mini-Minor (£497).

Surprisingly, the paintwork, and general finish standards, were better on the cheap-and-cheerful Herald S than they had been on the first Heralds, probably because the start up of production coincided with the commissioning of the new assembly hall at Canley.

But it was all to no avail. Although no separate figures are available to quantify the gamble, it seems that very few Herald S models were ever sold. Although build dragged on through the first year of Herald 1200 production, the S never found a market, and this type of cost-cutting expedient was never tried again.

In any case, in 1961 far more important events took place at Canley. First of all, the Leyland takeover was confirmed, and next, the Herald 1200 was announced. It was the start of the Herald's great come-back, which deserves a complete chapter to itself.

Facts and figures: Herald (now familiarly known as the '948 Herald')

General specification

All Heralds and Vitesses built between 1959 and 1971 were based on the same design, and engine layout/chassis/body structure. The following features were common throughout the range of models: Separate box-section steel chassis frame, with front-mounted engine/transmission, and rear chassis-mounted final drive unit. All bodyshells were in pressed steel, of welded *and* bolted-together construction; main sections were—floor/tail, scuttle/screen, bonnet/front wings, doors, and roof panel.

On this basis, saloon, coupé, convertible and estate styles were available on Heralds (depending on individual models), but only saloons and convertibles were commercially available on Vitesses.

Independent front suspension, by coil springs, wishbones, telescopic dampers, and anti-roll bar. Rack-and-pinion steering.

Independent rear suspension by transverse leaf spring, radius arms and telescopic dampers; swing axles on most models, but lower wishbones location on Vitesse Mk II models.

Girling brakes, all drum on 948 and 1200 models, optional front discs on 1200s, standard front discs/rear drums on 12/50s, 13/60s and all Vitesse models. Minor differences between models.

Wheelbase, all models, 91.5 in. (232 cm).

In the spring of 1962, these record shots were taken of the prototype four-door Herald. At the front there was no change, except that the front doors were appreciably shorter than on two-door cars, and they had frames around the top of window glasses

At the rear of the four-door, the changes were more obvious, for there was a modified rear quarter, and rather angular openings for the rear doors

Herald

Built	March/April 1959 to January 1964
Number built	100,275—76,860 saloons (including S), 15,153 Coupés, and 8262 Convertibles
Chassis numbers	G1 to G73751 inclusive (saloons, including 'S' with single-carb engines) GY1 to GY11392 inclusive (twin-carb saloons) Y1 to Y23248 inclusive (Coupés and Convertibles)

Basic price on introduction:

Saloon	£495	(Total £702)
Coupé	£515	(Total £731)
Twin-carb saloon	£520	(Total £737)
Convertible	£540	(Total £766
Saloon 'S'	£457	(Total £649)

Saloon specification
Engine 4-cyl., in-line, cast-iron cylinder block and cylinder head, with three crankshaft main bearings. Bore, stroke and capacity 63 × 76 mm, 948 cc (2.48 × 2.99 in., 57.9 cu. in.) Single carb engine, CR 8.0:1, one Solex downdraught carb. 34.5 bhp (net) at 4500 rpm. Maximum torque 48 lb ft at 2750 rpm.

Transmission Final drive ratio 4.875:1. Overall gear ratios 4.875, 7.09, 11.99, 20.82, reverse 20.82:1. Synchromesh on top, third and second gears. 13.5 mph/1000 rpm in top gear.

Suspension and brakes 8 × 1.25 in. front drum brakes, 7 × 1.25 in. rear drums. 5.20-13 in. tyres on 3.5 in. rim bolt-on steel disc wheels.

Dimensions Length 12 ft 9 in.; width 5 ft 0 in.; height 4 ft 4 in. Front track 4 ft 0 in.; rear track 4 ft 0 in. Unladen weight 1764 lb.

Coupé specification As for saloon, except for: CR 8.5:1, 2 SU carburettors. 45 bhp (net) at 5800 rpm. Maximum torque 49 lb ft at 3000 rpm.

Transmission Final drive ratio 4.55:1. Overall gear ratios 4.55, 6.62, 11.20, 19.45, reverse 19.45:1. 14.0 mph/1000 rpm in top gear.

Dimensions Height 4 ft 3.25 in. Weight 1736 lb.

Twin-carb saloon specification As for single-carb saloon, but with twin-carb engine, and transmission ratios, of Coupé.

Convertible specification As for saloon, except for: Convertible body style, twin-carb engine, and 4.55:1 final drive ratio. Unladen weight 1750 lb.

Herald 'S' specification As for single-carb saloon, or (optional) as for twin-carb saloon, except for simplified equipment.

Chapter 5
1200 and 12/50: reputation revived

If it was the original 948 cc Herald which nearly killed-off Standard-Triumph, it was certainly the 1200 and 12/50 models which led the revival. Naturally there were many other factors involved in the financial upheavals of 1960 to 1963, but the spate of takeovers, the opening and closing of new facilities, and the general re-structuring of the Standard-Triumph business was all done with the Herald in mind.

After he had left the company, Alick Dick once said, in a radio interview, that the main reason for Standard-Triumph's financial crisis at the end of 1960 was that they couldn't build Heralds quickly enough. In fairness, it would have been more accurate to say that it was impossible to *sell* Heralds fast enough.

Quite simply, unless they could cut back drastically on their expenses, and reduce the overall size of their business, and its workforce, Standard-Triumph needed to sell more cars to stay alive after 1960. Without the timely arrival of Leyland Motors on the scene, with a takeover proposal, it seems unlikely that they could have done this. Without the intervention of Leyland, the creditors might have closed in, there might never have been a Herald 1200, certainly not a Vitesse 1600, and the whole company might have closed down.

As is now well known, Leyland's offer was made public in December 1960, and was accepted, and completed, by the spring of 1961. There were top management changes both before, and immediately after, these events. In December 1960 Lord Tedder, the company's chairman since 1954, retired (he was 70 years old), and his place was taken by Alick Dick. Shortly after this, Martin Tustin gave up his post as the company's general manager, and went off to New York to become the boss of Standard-Triumph Inc., in the USA.

Jumping ahead a little, to the weeks immediately after the Herald 1200 had appeared, Leyland Motors moved in to take over complete control of Standard-Triumph, with Sir Henry Spurrier becoming chairman, and Donald Stokes, Stanley Markland and Sidney Baybutt (respectively sales, engineering, and financial specialists) also joining the board.

The Herald 1200 project, however, had begun to take shape as soon as the Herald was finalized, for Harry Webster knew that, ideally, more power and torque were needed. The Herald saloon, after all, weighed 70 lb more than the Pennant which, effectively, it displaced.

The engine, however, was not going to be easy to enlarge, for it had been designed, way back in 1952, to be an 803 cc/948 cc unit, and there was little 'elbow-room' in the cylinder block casting for stretch. As the engine was already undersquare (in other words, the bore dimension was less than the stroke—63 mm compared with 76 mm), only an enlargement to the bore was thought to be justified.

Recent interviews with engineers have also suggested that the position of the boring and honing tools in the transfer line machinery had not been changed since the arrival of the Standard Little Nine of the early 1930s! However, much of the SC engine's transfer line tooling had been newly-installed in 1955, in

ABOVE *The massive new Canley assembly allowed more derivatives, of better-built, Herald family cars to be built. It was opened in the winter of 1960/61, though this shot was taken several years later. Nowadays, alas, it is a big parts store for Unipart, cars not having been assembled there since 1980*

CENTRE *Herald assembly also took place in the Australian subsidiary company during the 1960s. Here the bodies are being built*

BELOW *By the late 1960s, Heralds were being assembled in among all the other cars in the family on the 'sideways' production line*

RIGHT *Donald Stokes, knighted in 1965, was one of the small group of Leyland Motors executives who turned round the Standard-Triumph business in the 1961–1964 period. He later went on to become chairman of British Leyland, until 1975*

place of old Mayflower tooling which *was* related to the Little Nine. . . .)

The designers looked at the layout of the unit, and swiftly concluded that it was not possible to enlarge the bore, and increase the engine size, by conventional means. There was stalemate until, as Harry Webster recalls:

'One night, at home, I woke up after some sort of a bad dream, couldn't get back to sleep, so I went off to my study, and it was then that I suddenly had this idea of moving the cylinder axes across, putting in a bit of *desaxé*, so that we could clear the holding down studs, and—bingo!—we could have the extra cylinder bore we needed.

'In fact I realized that with a stroke increase as well we could eventually get up to 1500 cc, but Alick Dick thought we should keep that up our sleeve for a time, and stick to the 1147 cc size at first. In detail, of course, there was much more to the stretch than that, but in essence the *desaxé* was the clincher.'

(*Desaxé*, incidentally, strictly means unbalanced, or out of true, which summarizes what was being done, in this case, for the centre line of the cylinder bores was moved, in space, 0.16 in. towards the camshaft side of the cylinder block, thus destroying the absolute symmetry, and ideal engine balance, of the unit.)

Rebuilders of this family of engines will know that it was a rather more complex re-shuffle than it might appear, even though there was no evidence of it from the outside of the unit. Perhaps *The Motor*'s summary of the changes was the most apt of all:

'As before, the cylinder bores are siamesed in pairs, but in order to accommodate the increase of 6.3 mm in each case, the disposition of their centre lines has been slightly modified; this has been achieved by a *desaxé* offset of 5/32 in. in the centre line of the bores, whilst the end bores

The Canley/Fletchamstead site in the mid-1960s, when the Herald's popularity was at its height. The modern assembly hall (with white walls) is in the centre right of this shot, while the big building to front right is the spares division and a gearbox machining shop. The separate building, lower left, was the 'strangers-excluded' design and experimental workshops complex. The main Coventry–Birmingham railway line is on the upper right, for this shot faces east, and Coventry's city centre is off the top of the shot

have been moved forwards and backwards by 5/32 in. and the inner pair brought closer together by a like amount. These changes have been effected without need for altering the cylinder head, induction or exhaust arrangements, apart, of course, from carburettor settings.'

(*The Autocar* quoted slightly different offset figures, but the general sense of the changes was exactly the same.)

In practical terms, to modify the boring and honing machinery was not as long-drawn-out, or as expensive, as was at first feared. Naturally a new cylinder block casting, and a new crankshaft, was required, but, as Harry Webster says:

'One day I found myself in the machine shop, and as I walked past the boring and honing tools . . . I saw the way the work was done. First they bored cylinders numbers one and three, and then two and four were done. All you had to do [to the machine settings] was to open up the stops, and move the boring and honing bars outwards in opposite directions.'

Strictly speaking, it was all wrong, especially as the new unit's engine balance would be less than ideal, and also because the new crankshaft encroached on space so much that the big end bearings had to be narrowed, by 0.18 in., to

0.91 in. In practical terms, however, there were no serious problems, and this is surely proved by the remarkable way that the engines could be race-tuned for the 1964/5 Spitfire race and rally programme. Only one extra precaution was needed, that being to specify copper-lead, indium-flashed shell bearings for big ends *and* mains, in place of the cheaper white metal bearings of the 948 cc units.

The result was a much more flexible, and torquey engine than before—for when you bore out an engine without making major changes to the cylinder head and breathing, torque usually benefits quite markedly, at lower engine speeds, because the gas-flow through the ports is speeded up considerably—that seemed to have lost nothing in refinement to its predecessors.

There was a real, and rather unexpected, bonus. Not only were the 1147 cc units more torquey than before, but significantly more powerful into the bargain. The improvement was such that it was immediately decided to drop the twin-carburettor tune for the time being, and reserve it for a sports car derivative (Bomb—or, as most of us know it—the Spitfire) at a later date.

Here are the comparative figures:

Engine size	**Peak power/rpm (bhp)**	**Peak torque/rpm (lb ft)**
948 cc (single carb)	34.5 at 4500	48 at 2750
948 cc (twin carb)	45 at 5800	49 at 3000
1147 cc (single carb)	39 at 4500	61 at 2250

Not only that, but the power and torque curves published by the factory in 1961, show that the 1147 cc engine offered more torque throughout the range, most especially between 1000 rpm and 3500 rpm, though the breathing efficiency (measured in BMEP terms) was actually worse above 3500 rpm, this being directly due to the use of valves and ports carried over from the smaller engine.

It was of course, only one of several important changes made to the Herald concept, all of which added up to a much more saleable proposition. Behind the engine, the same gearbox was used, but the overall gearing was raised considerably by the use of a new 4.11:1 final drive ratio for all types—saloon, Coupé, Convertible, and Estate car—instead of the 4.875:1 ratio of the single-carb 948 cc model, and 4.55:1 of the twin-carb models. At 70 mph, therefore, an 1147 cc engine was turning over at 4460 rpm (just about the power peak), compared with the frantic 5190 rpm of the single-carb 948 cc model.

The body construction, and general detail of the shells, was much as before, though this was not for want of a great deal of talking, and negotiation, on behalf of management. The built-up concept worked remarkably well (other body engineers, from rival concerns, still express surprise to the author that it was viable), but it was expensive, time-consuming to produce, and not as stiff as the quality-conscious engineers would like.

Management was not happy with the build quality of the shells produced by Mulliners, and even by the summer of 1959 they were threatening to withdraw the contract, and place it elsewhere. By the end of 1959, too, Pressed Steel Co. had overcome their tooling and production overload, sensed that Standard-Triumph might be open to negotiations, and asked if they could quote for taking over the body building business.

This had major implications on the expansion of premises in Liverpool, especially as the takeover of Hall Engineering (who later expanded considerably—their first overall body production contract being for the TR4, announced in September 1961); however, it was seriously considered, even to the extent of discussing which tooling and sections should be transferred to Pressed Steel, and in what order.

(For the record, Joseph Sankey Ltd, of Wellington, would have been first, Forward Radiator second, and the Hall Engineering facilities third. . . .)

Alick Dick had discussions with Joe Edwards, who was Pressed Steel's chief executive, in the spring of 1960, about timing, about costs, and about the need for completely re-tooling certain sections, such as the scuttle assembly, but it was

Self-explanatory display advertising for the Herald 1200's tiny turning circle, dating from the mid-1960s

months before a firm financial quote was received. By the time it arrived—in the autumn of 1960—Standard-Triumph were in deep trouble, and the £810,000 cost could not be met. For better, or for worse, therefore, the sectioned shell construction would have to remain.

In the meantime, however, the Tile Hill factory had been purchased from Fisher & Ludlow/BMC, and the big new assembly hall at Canley was also coming on stream. There was every chance that build quality would improve, even without changing the design.

Alick Dick, indeed, made several telling remarks, when he reported to his board in January 1961 about the state of negotiations with Leyland Motors. Leyland and Standard-Triumph were both very nervous about the company's financial situation, but Dick stated that he was more confident about prospects for the summer of 1961. His reasons were:

1 Quality had greatly improved.
2 There had been no Herald Convertible in 1960.
3 A larger engined Herald was to be introduced, with an increased specification, but a relatively small price rise.
4 A 'face-lift' Herald, at a cheaper price (the Herald S) was to be introduced in February 1961.
5 A Herald estate car was to be introduced with the 1200s.
6 The UK credit squeeze, imposed in April 1960, was now easing.

These remarks, firmly minuted, might have been as much for Leyland's directors to read, and to impress them, as to state any new developments of which other directors were not aware, but at least they summarized what the revised Herald range was all to be about.

The revised machine, to be known as Herald 1200, made its bow in April 1961, just two years after the very first Herald of all had been seen by the motoring public. Saloon, coupé and convertible styles were available at once, but a new estate car type was not actually launched for another three weeks. This was to allow the company two bites at the available publicity, and to let the press, and the public, assess the estate car on its own.

Visually, there were very few changes, and none at all to the general style, and pressed body panels. Most obvious was the use of rubber faces for the bumper strips (early Heralds were merely painted, as was the Herald S), and there was now a bright metal strip around the windscreen glass. The boot lid was now badged with the legend 'Herald 1200'.

The most important changes were to the interior. The rear seat squab (backrest) was now fixed in position, so that access through to the boot area was no longer possible. For all UK, and USA models, there was a smart new full-width wooden facia panel, with a lockable glove box lid (other marks retained their pressed fibre finish for the time being), and the 948 cc car's grey plastic, for the steering wheel, and switchgear, had given way to gloss black, which looked much smarter. All cars shared the same facia style (no unique set up for the Coupé, or the Convertible, anymore) with a single instrument, the speedometer, which also incorporated a fuel gauge.

The floor carpets were still moulded to shape, but their quality was higher. Seats, too, had been redesigned, with much thicker squabs and cushions. No sign remained of the plastic fold-down oddments basket or 'chip basket'.

All in all, the Herald 1200 looked, felt, and drove, like a much better car, and if ever a car was to claw back the company's image to respectability, this was it. It was certainly needed, for in the spring of 1961 the company's fortunes were at a low ebb. The TR3A production line had ground to a halt, and the Ensign/Vanguard cars were selling very slowly indeed. Which was precisely what Leyland's Sir Henry Spurrier told the board of directors when he became its chairman in May 1961:

'The company, at the moment, relies entirely on the Herald, and there is nothing to supplement this in the near future . . .'—by this time, of course, the last of the Pennant/Triumph 10 cars was long gone, and very few light vans were being produced. Things looked quite desperate.

LUCAS

But not for long. It was almost as if, when the public saw that Leyland had arrived, and were determined to turn the company round, that the Herald 1200's reputation began to grow steadily. The Estate car version, launched in the first week of May 1961, was another step along the way to credibility. The shape of this version was exactly as one might have expected, for Michelotti's crisp and sharp-edged style lent itself to an ideal 'square-back' estate style.

Behind the doors, which were exactly like those of the saloon, the Estate car had long, single-piece, side windows. The tailgate, was a large single-piece pressing, hinged at its roof edge, and supported, when open, by struts on each side of the glass. The rear bench seat was naturally arranged to fold down, but surprisingly enough the cushion itself did not swing forward to allow it to be flat. Nevertheless, there were seven sturdy rubbing strips on the load floor, and the back of the squab, to allow bulky loads to be slid in or out easily.

The estate car had several interesting technical details. Although the chassis design was unchanged, there was a stiffer transverse rear leaf spring, and fatter, 5.60-section, tyres, still on the same 3.5 in. wheel rims. The gear ratios were unaltered, but it was interesting to see that the big roof panel was of thicker steel

LEFT *1200 engine and gearbox – compare these with the original 948 cc assembly in the previous chapter. The bellhousing is now separate from the gearbox casing, and there was a different type of air cleaner*

LEFT BELOW *The Herald 1200 engine bay, viewed from above, now having a simple carburettor air cleaning casing, and pressed steel side curtains to the engine compartment itself*

BELOW *Worm's eye view of the Herald/Vitesse/Spitfire/GT6 type of independent front suspension, showing the anti-roll bar mountings, the rack-and-pinion mount positions, and the wide spacing of the lower wishbones*

than that of the saloons, to impart more stiffness—19 gauge (0.040 in.) instead of 20 gauge (0.036 in.). The roof, of course, was bolted down to the rest of the structure, by three fixings at each rear quarter, three across the windscreen header rail, and one to each centre pillar.

A new petrol tank location was needed, because of the load floor arrangements, and this was a nine-gallon container, tucked away under the rear load floor, close to the spare wheel. Because of its shape, and position, there was no way that the simple reserve pick-up arrangement could be provided.

The real attraction of all these 1200s, of course, was the improved quality allied to their prices. Compare them, for instance, with the superseded 948 cc models:

Total UK prices: April/May 1961

Herald S	£664
Herald 948 cc saloon	£702
Herald 948 cc coupé	£731
Herald 948 cc convertible	£766
Herald 1200 saloon	£708
Herald 1200 coupé	£736
Herald 1200 convert.	£776
Herald 1200 estate	£799

There were other interesting details. The Herald S, newly launched in February 1961, carried on, unadorned, and with its 948 cc engine, and while the saloons and Coupés normally had duo-tone paintwork, the Convertibles and Estates did not. It was also instructive to look under the bonnet, and see the pressed steel splash guards, or inner wheel-arches, which kept water and filth out of the engine bay; this was a great improvement on the original arrangement, or rather the lack of it, and had actually been phased in on the 948 cc models from 1960.

Of the four different Herald 1200s, the Coupé struggled hardest to make its mark. Perhaps it was altogether too much of a compromise—not sporting enough, or light enough, to be a proper sports coupé, not roomy enough to be a full four-seater. It was also actually slower, and less accelerative, than the original brand of coupé. Like the Convertible, it lost out in the rationalization process, with less horsepower, and fewer instruments. . . .

In any case, the Coupé had been mildly restyled in the roof area, from June 1960, when a ridged type of roof quarter panel took over from the previous plain expanse of painted metal. There were several good reasons for doing this, but the most important was undoubtedly to make the roof sub-assembly easier, and cheaper, to produce.

Even at first it sold very slowly, and once the Spitfire sports car became available it lost its appeal almost entirely. Factory figures show 2392 built in 1961, 1494 in 1962, 830 in 1963, and only 603 in 1964. Forty or 50 a month were being produced in mid-1964, which was clearly not viable—the last two cars were produced in October 1964.

A fascinating survey in *The Autocar* of 26 May 1961, produced by Midlands Editor Edward Eves, summarized all the unsung development changes which had gone into the Herald in the first two years of its career. Apart from the addition of pressed steel side-curtains to the engine bay, already mentioned, there had been improved water sealing around the screen pillars, the change to rubber suspension bushes instead of the original nylon (which squeaked), a cure for very smelly moulded carpets, extra stiffening panels on the scuttle near the outside corners, to stiffen it up, the introduction of hydrostatic, self-adjusting, clutch control, and better-built, quieter, transmissions.

Many of these, no doubt, would have been picked up by the engineers in a more protracted development period, but some of the changes, unfortunately, were made because the performance of mass-produced components did not match up to those produced for prototype purposes only.

My friends (colleagues, later) on *The Autocar* wrote a very interesting test report about an early 1200 saloon, and they were clearly impressed by the improvements. Perhaps it was significant that they, along with other observers, had begun to feel uneasy about the cars' 'on-the-limit' handling, for the following comments are apposite:

Even by the mid-1960s, there had been no major changes to the Herald's layout, as this 1967 shot confirms

'When the limit of adhesion is approached there is a positive but easily controlled change to oversteer. . . . This oversteer increases markedly if the throttle is closed while cornering fast. In wet weather it was found that this characteristic was more marked, particularly if tyre pressures were allowed to fall below the recommended settings . . . it was decided that with only two people aboard it is preferable to place luggage in the rear seat of the car rather than in the boot. . . .'

By the test reporting standards of the day, where comment was often mealy-mouthed, and one needed inside knowledge to see what was really thought, this meant that there was unease about the rear suspension. Such opinions were to become established, and more and more strongly repeated, in the years to come.

The Autocar's saloon was not as lively as *The Motor*'s Convertible, which could get up to 60 mph in 23.9 seconds, but both cars had top speeds of about 75 mph, and both averaged between 31.5 and 33.5 mpg. The cars , in other words, were finally looking right for their market.

Even so, it took time for the public to become convinced, and to start buying more Heralds again. The fact that there was another management upheaval in August/September 1961 could not have helped. Virtually all the 'Old Guard' of Standard-Triumph's directors, Alick Dick included, were ousted by Leyland, Stanley Markland became managing director, and along with Donald Stokes began the gritty job of slimming management down to size, while building up confidence for the future. Harry Webster and George Turnbull, two very important influences on the Herald, and all its derivatives, were finally elected board members in May 1962.

It is something of a miracle that the Herald family continued to expand, and improve, for it was in the 1961/62 period that the Spitfire was approved for production, that styling and basic engineering of the new Triumph 2000 saloon was finalized, and that work began on the front-wheel-drive 'Ajax'. The last project, covered in more detail in chapter 12, was considered as a direct replacement for the Herald at first.

During that winter, Herald assembly was cut from 925 cars a week, to a mere 750 a week, which equates to 39,000 a year, a far cry from the 160,000 a year target mentioned a year earlier. All sorts of ways were considered to freshen up its appeal, ranging from the proposal to produce a quick facelift 'based on the front end of the new "Atom"', which was quickly abandoned (but only until 1967 . . .), and to

CARRIER
SEVEN

the go-ahead for a project which was soon to become the 12/50.

Harry Webster celebrated his very first meeting as a board director, in May 1962, by saying that a twin-carburettor version of the 1200 engine could be available as an optional extra on the Coupé, and possibly the Convertible, but Stanley Markland wondered if this would kill demand for existing single-carb 1200s. Even though such an engine was soon to be standard on the Spitfire, it was never, in fact, made available for a Herald, and after this initial comment, appears to have been abandoned completely.

In the meantime, the first Herald saloon to have four doors had been completed in the experimental workshops, and the Herald Courier van had been put on sale. Although Sir Henry Spurrier later complained that there was no four-door Herald in production, this easy-to-produce derivative was never tooled up in the UK, and the prototype, and the designs, were eventually sold to the Standard Motor Products of India subsidiary, where it went into production as the Standard Herald, later the Standard Gazel. There is more detail of this model, at the end of the chapter.

The Courier was launched in February 1962, at the same time as the revamped van version of the obsolete Standard 8/10/Pennant range. The Courier (it had been the 'Carrier' at the prototype stage) was effectively an estate car shell, but without side windows, and with a wooden rear floor, with a detachable forward section. This could be removed, and an optional rear seat fitted. It was fitted with the plain Herald S grille, but had 4.5 in. wheel rims with 5.60-13 in. tyres. Those wide-rim wheels would be very useful as 'homologation' items for the Vitesse and Spitfire rally cars in the years to come.

ABOVE *Amphicar, and the Herald connection here is that this strange amphibious device was powered by a Herald 1200 engine, positioned behind the seats*

LEFT *The Herald Carrier was the name in this shot, but before launch at the beginning of 1962 that name was changed to Courier. Names don't matter – either way it was the Herald van, really an estate car without windows, no passenger seat, and wooden floor boards. The 'Seven' next to it was the 7 cwt van, the last of a long series which had been produced on the basic Standard 8/10/Pennant running gear and bodyshell*

Because it was a commercial vehicle, it was not subject to purchase tax, so superficially at least it was good value at £525. By comparison the ancient-design Standard 7 cwt van, now with the sharp-winged Pennant wing pressings, sold for only £430.

The Courier, however, was not a success. Like its passenger car relations, it was still quite expensive, compared with its competitors from Ford and BMC, and it never sold well. By the beginning of 1964, only two years after its launch, production was down to between 60 and 80 vehicles a month, which was quite derisory. The Courier, like the Coupé, therefore, was dropped in October 1964, after a very short life.

By 1962, however, there was real hope for the Herald family, and in 1963 a genuine recovery was under way. Strangely enough, the Herald 1200, as such, never even approached the achievements of the 948 cc car in 1960, and never bettered its own first-year total of 44,952 cars, but Canley itself was greatly boosted by the arrival of the 12/50, the Vitesse, and the Spitfire models. For 1961–2, the first year of control by Leyland, 66,807 cars were built at Canley, but this rose to 86,553 in 1962–3, and in the following year (with the new Triumph 2000 adding its quota) it surged ahead again, to 107,284.

For the 1200, the optional front disc brake kit, from the autumn of 1961, helped a bit, and so did the unexpectedly small price rise imposed during the summer of 1962. The rise was quite essential, in fact, for after the business had been slimmed down, and several hundred staff had been dismissed, the accountants did all their costing sums again, concluding that at the current depressed rate of production, every Herald was still being sold at a £10 loss! This would have been distressing for any businessman to learn, but was almost treated as an insult by the pragmatic Markland and Donald Stokes—the rise, merely to cover costs, followed immediately!

Within two years, however, the Herald 1200 had already reached its peak, in development

YDU 205

FDU 944C

terms. Though the saloon was to continue in production until the end of 1970, very few further changes, and no styling improvements, were ever made. The three-car range (saloon, Convertible, and Estate car) survived intact until the autumn of 1967, when the 13/60 was launched (see chapter 9), and immediately gave way to the new derivatives.

In the meantime, the company had developed an up-market Herald model, effectively to fill the gap between the 1200 and the Vitesse 1600. The up-rating of the engine, first proposed to the board in December 1961, went ahead, and by the autumn of 1962 it was tentatively given a title: Herald Gold Star. This name was never taken up by the sales departments, and when the definitive model was launched in March 1963, it reverted to the workaday title '12/50'.

Why 12/50? It was a reasonable compression of the philosophy of the car and its engineering: a 1200 model, with a 51 bhp (net) engine. On the other hand, there was more to the change than this, for the new derivative also had a fold-back sunshine roof, and upgraded trim.

In showroom terms, the new roof, by Weathershields, was a real sales point, as it was the very first to be fitted as standard equipment, to a British car, for some years. Other changes and improvements were the use of a new small-mesh radiator grille, a leathercloth-covered roll over the top of the facia panel, and the standardization of the heater and screen wash equipment (which were extra-cost items in the 1200). Even so, one still had to pay £8.31 for duo-tone paintwork, which most people wanted, and £6.04 for white-wall tyres, which few did.

LEFT *Nearly ten years of Herald 1200s, showing how nothing really changed in that decade. YDU 205 was pictured in 1961, as a pre-launch shot . . .*

LEFT BELOW . . . *while FDU 944C was a 1965 model . . .*

BELOW . . . *and GWK 880D was built in the summer of 1966*

Mechanically, the chassis and suspension of the 12/50 was virtually the same as that of the 1200, except that the 9.0 in. Girling front disc brakes, optional on other Heralds, were standard. All 12/50s, of course, had the stiffened up chassis frame—coded 'Star' in the design departments—which had been phased in at chassis number GA 80001 on 1200s. This frame was commonized, except for a few details relating to engine mountings, with that designed especially for the Vitesse 1600. When the Vitesse was launched (see the next chapter), the same type of frame was then fitted under the current, and all future, Heralds.

The engine produced 51 bhp (net) at 5200 rpm, and the published curves showed that it produced more torque from 2000 rpm upwards. The torque peak was 63 lb ft at 2600 rpm (compared with 61 lb ft at 2250 rpm), which disguised the fact that there was about 20 per cent more torque between 4000 and 5000 rpm, where an enterprising driver most wanted it.

This had been achieved without enlarging the 1147 cc engine (Harry Webster was still holding that back . . .), but by increasing the compression ratio from 8.0 to 8.5:1, fitting a new pump-type Solex B30 PSEI carburettor, redesigning the exhaust/inlet manifold 'hot-spot' to cut down on heat transfer and—most importantly—fitting the high-lift Spitfire camshaft.

For all this, Triumph asked for £635 (there had been a reduction in purchase tax in April, and again in November, 1962), which compared with £579 for the Herald 1200, and £735 for the Vitesse 1600. It was an attractive package, and the car sold well, for 53,267 were to be made before the autumn of 1967 when it gave way to the 13/60, its natural successor. This was quite remarkable when it is remembered that only a saloon version was ever offered.

The 12/50 was significantly, if not dramatically, quicker than the 1200, as independent

In 1961, the original Herald 1200 had a smart wooden facia and a shaped gear knob . . .

road test figures showed. A top speed of 78–80 mph, and 0–60 mph acceleration of 23 sec. was typical. Even so, it was a car that had to be urged along before it gave of its best, and the Leyland-based management (who were much more impressed by good 10–30 mph performance in top gear, than in a high maximum speed—throwbacks to truck performance, if ever I saw one!) were not as impressed.

Booming Triumph sales, however, all helped Donald Stokes' confident statements and forecasts to ring true. As he said, in an interview with *The Motor* in May 1963:

'We're sure there's a niche for us in the small car market. There will always be a place for a vehicle that appeals to a more discriminating buyer than the average volume-produced car because, for example, it handles better and has a better finish. Ours is a little more expensive than some of the volume-produced cars. . . . It's a fact that the guarantee costs are a true indication of your quality. . . . Our guarantee costs have come down steadily and consistently ever since we started our quality control campaign. . . . We want to build good motor cars with a good performance in the medium sort of bracket. I think that the sales we are achieving at the moment prove that there is a place in the market for us, and we're improving our share of the small-car market.'

There was no huff and puff in this interview, for the facts were on show for the world to see. Spearheaded by the Herald, Standard-Triumph were on the way back. A very important factor, however, had been the birth of the six-cylinder Vitesse, and this deserves a chapter to itself.

The Standard Gazel

Earlier in this chapter, I mentioned the four-door Herald, and I should now relate what happened to it. By the end of 1963, the existing Herald was being assembled in the company's Indian subsidiary, at the rate of 4000 cars a

. . . but soon the gear knob was a round black plastic ball, more comfortable to handle. Otherwise, no change for some years

4421 HP

LEFT *The very first Herald 1200 estate prototype had a duo-tone colour scheme*

LEFT BELOW *The 1200 estate was an extremely practical machine, and handsome in its own way*

RIGHT *Clever composite shot, showing the way the lift-up tailgate of the Herald estate was articulated*

year. Expansion to 5000 a year was expected shortly, as the 1147 cc engine had just been introduced.

In the meantime, the four-door project had been abandoned in the UK, and the style had been sold to India, where Standard Motor Products of India Ltd proceeded to lay down their own tooling.

Because the car was locally assembled, but totally manufactured in India for some time, it was a strange hybrid at all times, and I regret that I have not been able to pinpoint the relevant start-up and close-down dates. In response to queries, the Indian company's manager, T. N. Ragunathan merely told me 'the car has been out of production for well over 10 years . . .' in a 1985 letter.

In fact, for local manufacture, the company always kept to the 948 cc engine, producing 35 bhp at 4800 rpm, with a 7.2:1 compression ratio, with the normal Herald gearbox ratios, but with final drive ratios of 4.875:1 or 4.55:1. The Standard Herald (*not* the Triumph Herald, please note) was essentially the same as the UK model, though the same basic bonnet shape and style as the 13/60 was later adopted. At a later date, the front end structure was changed, so that the whole nose did not tilt forward in conventional Herald fashion, but a separate rear-hinged bonnet was used. By this time, even the two-door roof line had been altered from UK-standard while the four-door machine had rather upright rear quarter styling to accommodate both doors, on the same chassis. The Standard Gazel was rather different. Not only did it use yet another version of the Vitesse bonnet pressings and front style, with single seven inch headlamps, and the indicator bulb squeezed up into the top corners, but it was badged as a Standard, and had the four passenger doors only. On the later Standard Heralds, there had been a four-door estate car, and this feature was also present in the Standard Gazel. The saloon version had a rather nondescript rear end, in which the fins were chopped off, and in which a different boot lid, and different low-mounted tail lamp assemblies were used. I have to say that I do not find these changes an improvement!

Underneath, too, in Mr Ragunathan's own words, there was a 'rigid differential' at the rear, while the catalogue merely mentions rear suspension as being by coil springs and an anti-roll bar. However, I now understand, from John Lloyd, that the car had a much modified rear chassis frame, and was fitted with a rigid 'live' rear axle, of the 10/Pennant type.

The Gazel, though advertised as a 'Small Big Car', was nevertheless basically equipped, for it had drum brakes all round, a long spindly gearlever (not the remote control installation of the Herald), a different facia style, and a full-width bench front seat. It was built in Madras, and as far as I know, no single example ever came over to the UK.

ABOVE *By the late 1960s Triumph were happy to advertise the Herald's tenth birthday in 1969, like this*

RIGHT *12/50 in the UK had a special small-mesh radiator grille and badge, and sunshine roof*

Herald 1200

Built February 1961 to June 1970
Number built 289,575—201,142 saloons, 5319 coupés, 43,295 convertibles, 39,819 estates.
Chassis numbers GA1 to GA249873 inclusive (all bodies with same prefix)
Basic and total price on introduction

Saloon	£499	(Total £708)
Coupé	£519	(Total £736)
Convertible	£544	(Total £772)
Estate car	£562	(Total £799)

Saloon specification
Engine: 4-cyl., in-line, cast-iron cylinder block and cylinder head, with three crankshaft main bearings. Bore, stroke and capacity 69.3 × 76 mm, 1147 cc (2.73 × 2.99 in., 70 cu in.). CR 8.0:1, one Solex downdraught carburettor. 39 bhp (net) at 4500 rpm. Maximum torque 61 lb ft at 2250 rpm. From November 1964 48 bhp (net) at 5200 rpm; maximum torque 62 lb ft at 2500 rpm.
Transmission Final drive ratio 4.11:1. Overall gear ratios 4.11, 5.74, 8.88, 15.42, reverse 15.42:1. Synchromesh on top, third and second gears. 15.7 mph/1000 rpm in top gear.
Suspension and brakes 8 × 1.25 in. front drum brakes, 7 × 1.25 in. rear drums. 5.20-13 in. tyres on 3.5 in. bolt-on steel disc wheels.
Dimensions Length 12 ft 9 in.; width 5 ft 0 in.; height 4 ft 4 in. Front track 4 ft 0 in.; rear track 4 ft 0 in. Unladen weight 1792 lb.

Coupé specification As for saloon, except for:
Dimensions Height 4 ft 3.25 in. Unladen weight 1736 lb.

Convertible specification As for saloon, except for: Convertible body style. Unladen weight 1764 lb. Estate specification as for saloon except for estate body style. 5.60-13 in. tyres on 3.5 in. rim wheels. Unladen weight 1890 lb.
NOTE: 9.0 in. diameter front disc brakes became optional on all Heralds from autumn 1961. With discs, the front track was 4 ft 1 in.

Herald 12/50

Herald 12/50
Built December 1962 to August 1967
Number built 53,267—all saloons
Chassis numbers GD1 to GD55689 inclusive.
Basic and total price on introduction
Sunroof saloon £525 (Total £635**)
**Note that Purchase tax levels had been reduced since the launch of the original Herald 1200 models.

Saloon specification As for Herald 1200, except for: Fabric sliding sunroof standard on every car. Engine CR: 8.5:1, 51 bhp (net) at 5200 rpm. Maximum torque 63 lb ft at 2600 rpm.
Brakes 9.0 in. front discs. Front track 4 ft 1 in. Unladen weight 1855 lb.

No coupé, convertible or estate versions of the 12/50 were ever officially produced.

LEFT *The Herald estate car, with back door open, and with backrest folded forward to increase the loading area*

ABOVE *This was no ordinary Herald convertible, but a short-wheelbase version, actually with a Spitfire chassis under the skin, first built towards the end of 1960. The author drove this car often, and reckons it was the best-handling 'Herald' ever built*

Chapter 6
The Vitesse project: Six into Four *will* go!

Although the original six-cylinder Vitesse was launched in May 1962, three years after the Herald had first been put on sale, it might have been ready considerably earlier than this. The traumatic corporate upheaval of 1961, and the financial drama which led up to this, has already been discussed. This certainly caused some delay, but another factor was the ever-changing nature of the forward-planning for new models, and—in particular—the 'Zebu' project.

The Zebu story really began in 1957, and first official mention of this came at a board meeting held in August of that year. On the occasion that Zobo got its official go-ahead, there was also talk of a new Zeta saloon, Michelotti-styled on the existing 10 hp/Pennant underpan and suspensions, for which it was thought that the first cars could be built in July 1959, and there was also discussion of Zebu.

At the time, Zebu was considered as a 1500/2000 cc saloon, with a straight-six overhead valve engine which was to be a direct evolution and development of the existing SC/future Herald four-cylinder unit. It was to have a separate chassis frame, for the same reason as the Herald had such a frame, the transmission was to be in unit with the final drive, at the back of the car, there was to be four-wheel independent suspension, and it had to be capable of accepting a pneumatic type of suspension springing when this was sufficiently well-developed.

Under the 'ever hopeful' heading came the statement that Standard would be styling the car (after the debacle of the Zobo 'bathtub' and the Pennant!), and that Pressed Steel Co. would be producing bodyshells. 'Job One' for this car was slated for March 1960.

Zebu, in effect, was to be a slightly smaller replacement for the Standard Vanguard III, itself due to be up-dated to 'Vignale' specification by the summer of 1958. When the car was in full production in 1960/1, it was hoped that about 30,000 a year would be built and sold; by the beginning of 1960 that forecast had slipped to 25,000 a year. This figure was low by—say—Ford and BMC standards, but would prove to be an over-optimistic figure when the car's eventual successor, the Triumph 2000, eventually went into full production.

The need for such a car had been spelt out repeatedly by Standard's sale force who, as early as 1955, had been asking for a 12 hp/14 hp car (under the old RAC Rating, this meaning a 1.5/1.8-litre car in current terms): 'as in our view this car is in the greatest demand'.

During 1958 and 1959, however, the Zebu project was always difficult to define, and difficult to develop. The styling gave endless trouble (it was the Zobo problem all over again), there were mechanical problems with the advanced chassis layout (the engineers found it difficult to make the drive line completely smooth and vibration-free), and over-riding everything was the fact that money for investment became more and more difficult to find. During 1959, after the Herald was put on sale, the 2-litre six-cylinder engine was slotted in to the Vignale Vanguard, together with a four-speed gearbox similar to that of the

TR3A, and the Luxury Six was ready for launch, as yet another 'interim' model, by the autumn of 1960.

In the meantime, the notion of slotting a six-cylinder engine into the structure of the Herald had begun to take shape. The car had not originally been intended to accept a six-cylinder engine, but Harry Webster's design and development engineers were so speedy, and so resourceful, that when the time came, they managed it without much fuss.

It was not, *definitely* not, a car which the sales departments wanted. As Harry Webster told me: 'It was crazy really. The M1 motorway had just opened [in November 1959], and I felt that I wanted a faster car to use on that road. I decided that we should put a two-litre six-cylinder engine into a Herald! We had a spare Herald Coupé in the workshops, we put a two-litre engine into it, blanked off first gear because the gearbox, and the axle for that matter, wouldn't take the torque, and I just used it, and liked it very much. . . . Then I gave it to our sales people to try, they eventually came to like it, so it went into production. Until the thing was *there*, in front of them, they didn't want it at all.'

In every way, then, the new project, which was given the code of 'Atom', was a Webster/Tustin/Turnbull invention. None of them ever looked for sales of more than 100 to 150 cars a week, and since new investment was likely to be low, this made it a potentially profitable model right from the start.

A long-running Standard-Triumph project in the late 1950s/early 1960s, was 'Zebu', which featured a separate chassis frame, a six-cylinder engine, and a rear-mounted transmission. Eventually it was cancelled, the Triumph 2000 project took its place, but in due course the Vitesse theme evolved from it

That first car, not registered until 1962 as 8278 VC, was a Coupé with a modified Herald bonnet at first, and carried the chassis number of X663. It was updated from time to time during the test and development period, but eventually got a true Vitesse-type chassis frame, which was coded 'Star', a 1.6-litre engine, and all the appropriate mechanical equipment.

When the author first came to know this car in 1961, it was affectionately known as the 'Kenilworth Dragster' (Harry Webster lived in Kenilworth . . .), was fitted with de-cambered rear suspension, and twin fuel tanks, one on each side of the boot space, to give a much extended fuel range. The combination of de-cambered rear suspension, and the extra fuel load when both tanks were well filled, made this car delightful to drive fast.

The 'lash-up' prototype was on the road early in 1960, and a tentative production programme of 'Atom' was discussed, when it was thought that up to 8500 might be sold in a full year. At this time it was, of course, definite that it would be badged as a Triumph, but the model name had not been settled. At this time, precisely, the twin-cam 'Sabrina' engined 'Zoom' sports car (which might have gone into production during 1961 if there had been enough money available . . .) was to have been called Triumph Vitesse! Ah well. . . .

During 1960, as I have already made clear, everything in the forward programme changed, and changed yet again. The Zebu programme staggered from crisis to crisis, and even though a mock-up was made, of a longer and wider four-door Herald bodyshell to go over the chassis and running gear, nothing was ever decided. By April it had been decided to put back its launch until late 1962, at the earliest, by September the company had been approached by American Motors of Detroit to consider assembling the Nash Rambler at Canley, but fitted with Vanguard Luxury Six engines and transmissions. At this point the Zebu programme was cancelled forthwith.

Once Zebu had been cancelled (and once it became clear that the Vanguard Six would not keep the company going for too long), the Atom project took on greater importance. In a classic 'shutting the stable door after the horse had gone' operation, it was then formally decided to build the mock-up of a six-cylinder, four-door Herald, this being months after the 'Kenilworth Dragster' had been put on the road! Tooling costs for the new bodyshell were estimated at a mere £400,000, and only £50,000 was supposedly needed for other machine tooling. In addition, another £60,000 was to be earmarked for the re-tooling of the chassis frame to the 'Star' layout.

BOTH ABOVE *Using an existing Herald coupé wooden body buck, Michelotti produced the new nose for the six-cylinder car which was eventually named Vitesse*

BOTH LEFT *In the autumn of 1959, with the 'Zebu' project tottering towards cancellation, this mock-up was speedily made, to see if a widened, lengthened, four-door Herald bodyshell could be used on a new chassis. It never advanced beyond this point, but the Vitesse project certainly arose from it*

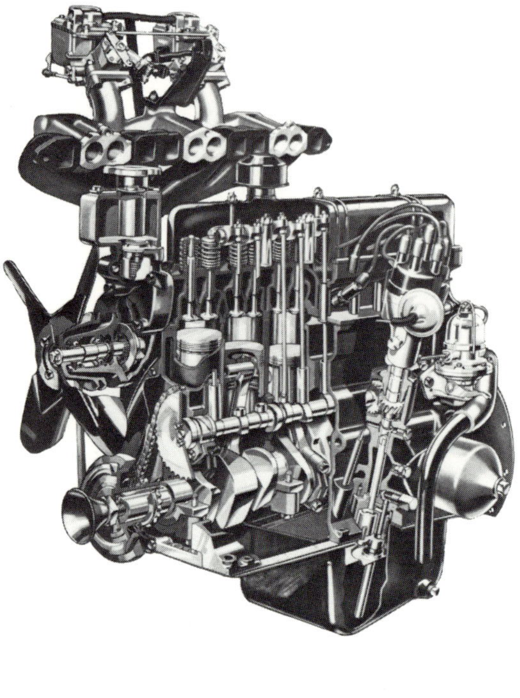

ABOVE *This picture dates from December 1960, and is of the first (Italian-registered) Vitesse prototype. There was no Vitesse coupé ever offered as a production car, though this would not have been difficult to arrange*

LEFT *The six-cylinder Vanguard engine, of 1998 cc, looked like this in cutaway form, and had siamesed cylinder bores. For the Vitesse, the bore dimension was decreased, the block was recored to give water-cooling all round, but the same type of semi-downdraught carburettors were retained*

BOTH RIGHT ABOVE *Two views of the 1596 cc six-cylinder Vitesse engine, which had twin semi-downdraught Solex carburettors. The family link to the four-cylinder Herald engine is obvious, for much of the machining was common*

In the next few weeks, the Michelotti studio produced the now well-known four-headlamp bonnet assembly, complete with slanting lamp installation, said to have an Oriental aspect by some observers, and the whole lift-up front end was re-engineered to make space for the very far forward mounting of the radiator, necessitated by the longer engine itself.

In March 1961, the 'Atom' project was completely defined, and approval was given by management, which was now under Leyland Motors control, even though new directors had not then joined the board. The target for announcement was at the Earls Court Motor Show of October 1961, but almost at once this was seen to be impossible, and the date was rescheduled for March 1962. In the event, even this was not feasible, and actual launch was in May 1962.

Although the specification was simplified in one respect—the idea of building it as a four-door car was dropped, for instance—it was potentially made more complex in another. Serious consideration was not only given to restyling the rear end of the bodyshell, but revising the interior too. Target price for the saloon was £560 (basic)—but the car would actually cost £608 when it was revealed. The only new bodyshell tooling required was for the bonnet assembly (this cost £70,000), while Sankeys were contracted to produce the new Star chassis frame at a tooling cost of £48,600; this frame, once ready, would be used under all Herald/Vitesse cars.

All the serious development, testing, and pavé work took place in 1961, even while tooling-up for the new frame went ahead. For the time being, Harry Webster's 'Kenilworth Dragster' put in much invaluable service, as did the first of the true 'ground-up' prototypes, a black and white saloon registered 1098 RW, and carrying chassis number X673. At this stage, certainly, one Atom estate car was built up—the body styles behind the scuttle and windscreen were, of course, exactly the same as the Herald—but there was never any serious intention to offer such a car in production. Right from the start, in fact, the sales departments were only willing to market saloons and convertibles. The idea of an Atom coupé, like the original lash-up, was superficially attractive, but since only 2392 Herald 1200 Coupés were sold in 1961, and 1494 in 1962, there was really no justification for persevering with the idea.

Frankly, Standard-Triumph were extremely lucky, that the six-cylinder engine could actually be fitted under the bonnet of the Herald style bodyshell, for it had never been intended for that purpose in the first place. Nor, for that matter, was it possible without making many changes to the chassis frame.

The story starts, therefore, with a complete revision of the frame, at the front to accom-

ABOVE *The Vitesse 1600 engine, as installed, complete with low-mounted air cleaner, and separate radiator header tank, inboard of the carburettors. The radiator has had to be moved all the way forward to make way for this bulky unit*

RIGHT ABOVE *Vitesse 1600 engine bay from the left side. Clearly, access to the electrical fittings is very straightforward*

FAR RIGHT *The white painted patches on this chassis show the improvements made to the basic Herald design, to make it suitable for use in the Vitesse application. Apart from judicious stiffening here and there, there had to be a cut-out around the transmission to allow an overdrive to be fitted when ordered. Front and rear brakes, too, were enlarged*

modate the engine, around the gearbox area to make provision for an optional overdrive installation (not offered, and never subsequently offered, for the Herald), and around the final drive casing to allow for a more sturdy casing, and to give more resistance to twisting caused by the increased torque. There were also local stiffening operations around the roots of the front outriggers, and the rear of the side members. The wheelbase and the basic wheel tracks, of course, were not changed, and the general layout of the frame, with its backbone members, and the separate bolt-on towers for the front suspension, was the same as before. Structurally, the big improvement was to the location of the final drive unit, and to the rear damper mountings; almost the same detail was applied to the rear of the Spitfire's frame, which was first seen a few months later.

As the gearbox itself could not be moved back along the line of the frame, the extra length of the engine had to be accommodated by allowing it to 'grow' further forward. The sump pan had to be stepped to let it clear the chassis crossmember, the cooling fan was very close to the cooling radiator, and the radiator itself was right up against the new grille and front bonnet panel. Nevertheless, there was so little space up front that the designers chose to position a separate radiator header tank above the engine, squeezing this between the tappet cover, and the air inlet ducting for the carburettors.

The basic suspension layout was exactly like that of the Herald, though rates and settings were changed to allow for the different weights and their distribution. At the front, however, there were 9.0 in. Girling disc brakes, and at the rear drum brake sizes had been increased, from 7.0 in. to 8.0 in. diameter.

The engine itself was a development of that already seen in the Vanguard Luxury Six, which had a capacity of 1998 cc. For Atom, and taking note of the fact that a new large saloon car was scheduled to follow it into production not much more than a year later, it was decided to use a new size, of 1596 cc. Compared with the 2-litre engine, this was done by using a smaller cylinder bore (66.75 mm instead of 74.7 mm) and recoring the cylinder block—this, incidentally, allowing cooling water to circulate all around those bores, whereas on the larger engine the bores had been siamezed.

The compression ratio was 8.75:1, and the same, unique, semi-down-draught Solex Type 32 PHI twin carburettors were used. The air

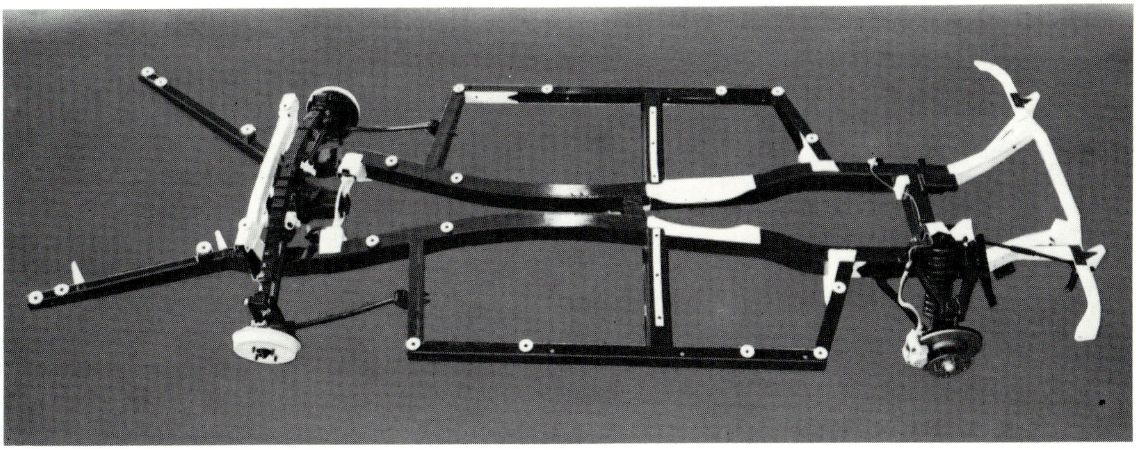

intake passages were tortuous, and cannot have helped the volumetric efficiency. Not even cold air was sucked in to the system, in any case, but warm air which had already come through the cooling radiator. This was then filtered through a low-mounted AC-Delco paper element air cleaner positioned underneath the carburettors, taken up between the carbs, then turned smartly through 180 degrees, and a slim pressed collector box, before getting into the carbs themselves.

Behind the engine, there was a new ribbed clutch housing, with a slave cylinder on the right side, and inside the existing gearbox casing there was a new set of delightfully close clutch ratios. The final drive ratio of 4.11:1 was unchanged, but compared with the Herald 1200, first gear had been raised from 15.42:1 to 12.06:1.

Behind the engine, the bodyshell's sheet metal was just the same in Atom as in the Herald 1200, and the only change to accommodation was that the boot compartment was made slightly smaller by the fitment of a larger (9 Imperial gallons, instead of 7 Imperial gallons) fuel tank. The trim level, and standard of the fittings, compared with the Herald 1200, was raised, but the car was still only equipped, in the first place, with one circular instrument, a speedometer which also contained a fuel contents gauge.

Externally, the requested rear end re-style had not been carried out, except for the use of a chrome-plated canopy over the numberplate. At the front the slanting four-headlamp style was obvious, and at front and rear there were new, extruded and anodized bumper bars, produced by the British Aluminium Co., and gleefully demonstrated to the press at the time the car was launched.

All cars were to have a duo-tone colour scheme, the contrasting colour being arranged to surround the headlamps and the front grille, and in long 'spears' along the flanks of the bodyshell, but not across the tail.

In the run up to the launch of the new model, it was necessary to choose a name. By the end of 1961, the twin-cam engine project had been abandoned, so the name Vitesse was applied to the 1.6-litre six-cylinder machine. It was, in any case, already a famous Triumph name, having already been used for a series of sleek 1930 sports saloons, at a time when the Triumph Motor Co. Ltd was still an independent concern.

(Later, of course, the name Vitesse would be applied to a high-performance version of the big Rover hatchback—but by this time Rover had taken over from Triumph in the BL, or Austin-Rover, scheme of things, and Herald/Vitesse enthusiasts had washed their hands of the affair.)

Number-noters, incidentally, were extremely puzzled by the registration numbers sported by the Vitesse cars used in some publicity pictures. Two of these numbers, as seen in *Autocar* of 25 May 1962, were 3 VC and 4 VC—but such numbers had already been seen on John

Sprinzel's and Mike Sutcliffe's 'works' TR4 rally cars in the Tulip rally. . . .

When the quartet of TR4s was assembled at Coventry under my direction, a series of distinctive numbers—3 VC, 4 VC, 5 VC and 6 VC—were acquired from the local licencing authority. Because it was 'fashionable' at the time, and because the front bumpers had in any case been removed, making normal plates difficult to use, these numbers found a home on the bonnet of the cars, with self-adhesive numerals and digits.

When the time came to take pictures of the publicity cars, which had not then been registered, a search was made for numberplates. In a corner of the press car garage, guess what should be available, but sets of conventional plates, made up unasked (because the 'system' demanded it at the factory, at the time) for the team rally cars? All of which explains the apparent duplication. Incidentally, cars were never driven on the public highway with the wrong plates affixed.

The Vitesse, when launched, got a very good reception from the motoring press, as well it might. It was, after all, the first new 'small six' from a British factory for many years, harking back, in some traditionalists' eyes, to cars like the *other* Triumph Vitesse, or even to cars like

RIGHT *When the Vitesse was launched in 1962, it had a very simple facia style, like that of the Herald 1200, though the standard of trim and furnishings was clearly more up-market*

RIGHT BELOW *Effective September 1963, the Vitesse was given this more comprehensive facia/instrument layout, which included a rev-counter (red-lined at 6000 rpm), and separate fuel and water temperature gauges. There was also a map pocket, low down in the passenger's foot well*

BELOW *For the Vitesse, a much more robust chassis 'bridge' was built across the rear to support the differential casing, and the dampers. The design, by the way, was almost exactly like that to be used in the new Spitfire sports car*

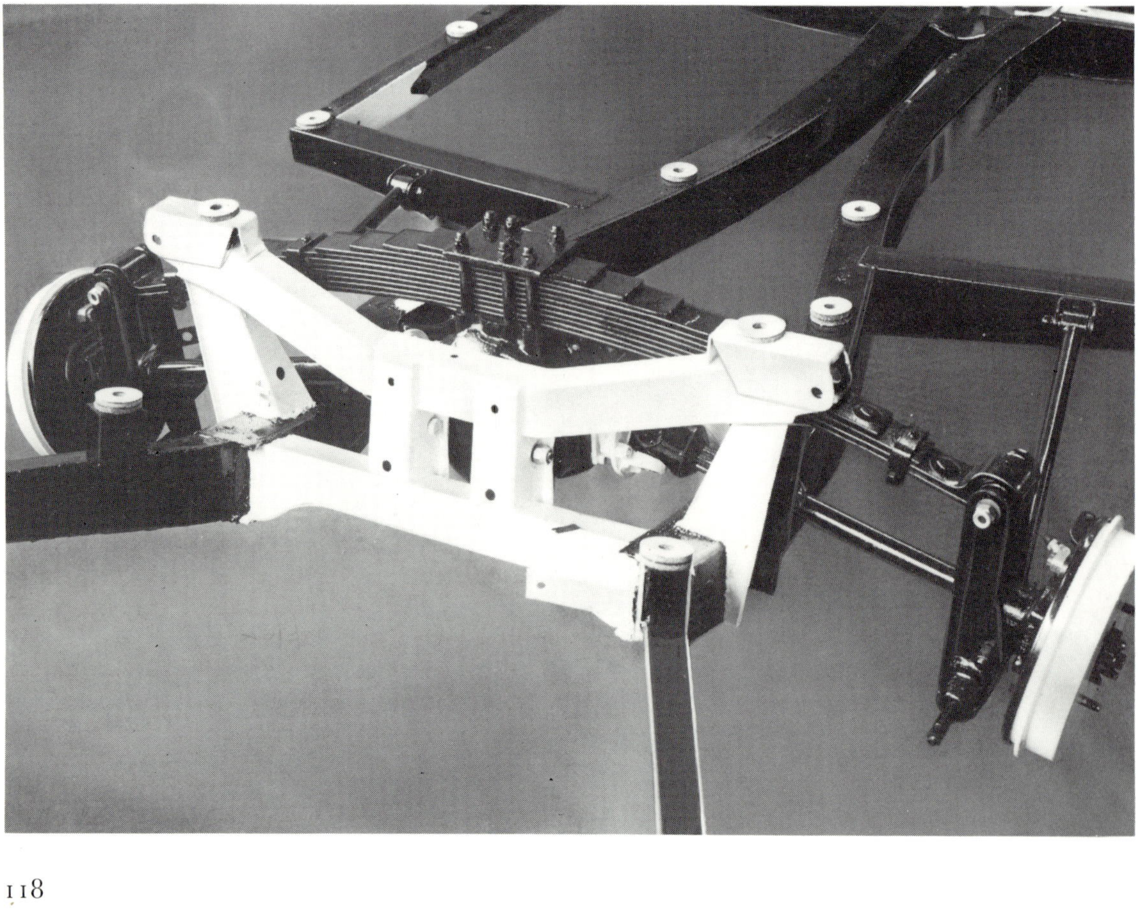

the Wolseley Hornet, the Triumph Scorpion, and similar Singers, Morris, and Austin models.

Not only was it an attractive little car (and, yes, let's not forget, it still was a small, compact, machine), but it promised to be a fast car too. Compared with the Herald 1200 saloon, the Vitesse weighed 2044 lb instead of 1792 lb, but had 70 bhp (net) instead of 39 bhp, the effective power weight ratio of the Vitesse being 77 bhp/ton instead of 49 bhp/ton. Because the gear ratios were closer together, and altogether more sporting, the Vitesse promised to be a fast little sports saloon.

Production of the Vitesse saloon and convertible models was already under way before they were publicly revealed, the first eight production cars being completed in April 1962, and by motor show time more than 250 cars were being assembled every week. This was already way ahead of the demand needed to make the Vitesse a profitable model, and as John Lloyd recalls: '. . . all the opposition to the Vitesse came from the sales department, who said they could never sell them. Harry and George Turnbull then said, "We're going to make them—you sell them now!", and ever afterwards the sales people couldn't get enough!'

The Motor's Vitesse test, of October 1962, typified the attitude of the specialist press to the new car headlining it a 'slim little 6-cylinder saloon', the testers summed up a searching report with these words:

Two men of the moment – Stanley Markland (Standard-Triumph's managing director from 1961 to the end of 1963) sitting in a Vitesse convertible, and talking to technical director Harry Webster

'The Vitesse has many attractions to counter several faults. It is only five feet wide, it can turn round without reversing in a road only 23 feet wide between kerbs, and it costs only £837 complete with heater. With compactness and cheapness of this order, its willing, smooth and rapid performance is both distinctive and attractive, making it very much a driver's car. . . .'

The 'several faults' included a clutch which slipped when abused, and a very 'spongy' brake pedal feel—both of which might have been due to faulty pre-test preparation—and complaint about tyre scrub at full lock. (But how can you get a 23 foot turning circle, which was even better than advertised, without a lot of that?) They also thought that the springing was too firm, and there were several vague comments about the handling ('fast driving is apt to see the driver putting on and taking off lock to some extent. . . .')

The only truly worrying detail was that the engine clearly had a very high octane requirement, and the factory was already aware of this problem. With the existing (original) design of cylinder head, and with a very shallow combustion chamber needed to produce an 8.85:1 compression ratio, there was always the likelihood of pre-ignition setting in.

The Vitesse 1600 was launched in May 1962, with saloon and convertible body options. Those publicity shots, however, confused number noters, for the supposed number plates – 3 VC and 4 VC – actually belonged to the 'works' TR4 rally cars of the period. 3 VC was always used by John Sprinzel, and 4 VC was Mike Sutcliffe's car which finished fourth in the Alpine rally of that year

The Motor's testers wrote that: 'Premium-grade petrol had an octane rating just high enough to satisfy our test car, but even a slightly below-average batch of this fuel would cause pinking during acceleration, or running-on after the ignition was switched off.' *That* was a problem the factory would have to live with for quite some time.

As to the performance the car, registered 9146 RW, and not fitted with the optional overdrive, achieved a mean maximum speed of 88.8 mph (5400 rpm, incidentally), 0–60 mph in 17.6 seconds, and an overall fuel consumption (over 1196 miles) of 25.1 mpg.

(Just to prove that fitment of the overdrive did more for relaxed high-speed cruising, but nothing for performance, *Autocar*'s test car, registered 1224 VC, reached 86.8 mph in overdrive top, 85.0 mph in direct top, 0–60 mph in 17.8 sec., and had an overall fuel consumption figure of 24.6 mpg.)

This performance was exactly as predicted by the engineers, and competitive with all its rivals, when the Vitesse was launched. However, from the spring of 1963, the Ford Cortina GT made its bow, and although it cost £14 more in two-door form, it had a top speed of 94 mph, and 0–60 mph acceleration in under 14 sec. Further, it proceeded to carve out an impressive competitions record, which the Vitesse did not. Something would have to be done.

The solution was almost immediately to hand. When the Triumph 2000 was launched in the autumn of 1963, it displaced the Standard Vanguard Luxury Six, with which it shared the same basic engine unit. The Vanguard's 1998 cc engine had been equipped with the same semi-downdraught carburettors as the Vitesse 1600, and had produced 80 bhp (net) at 4400 rpm. The 2000's engine had twin horizontal Zenith-Stromberg carbs, and other improvements, and developed 90 bhp at 5000 rpm. Further, at one time there was to have been a Triumph 1600, with the Vitesse-size engine, and the twin Zenith-Strombergs. . . .

At a board meeting in May 1964, Harry Webster stated that experiments had already been carried out 'with the 2000 carburettors and manifolds on the Vitesse engine'. The extra cost to the company, he said, was just £1 a car, and the result was an extra 13/14 bhp. It was not surprising, therefore, that the board immediately decided to authorize the improvement, which was actually phased in, on the production line, from chassis no. HB 28061, from mid 1965.

The results were positive, but the improvement was not dramatic. One puzzle was that Harry Webster's 'extra 13 to 14 bhp was never actually advertised by Standard-Triumph, the other was that the revised cars didn't feel completely different.

When *The Autocar* tested a 'Mk 2' 1600 Convertible in the summer of 1965, they reported a top speed of 91 mph (paradoxically, in overdrive third gear, not in direct or overdrive top!), and 0–60 mph acceleration in 15.5 seconds, the latter figure being 15 per cent better than before. Fuel economy had also improved—their overall figure was 25.8 mpg—so it was certain that the change had been worthwhile.

As with the 12/50, however, this Vitesse was something of a 'top-end' car. The testers commented that:

'The same power and torque figures are quoted . . . yet this convertible proved considerably quicker off the mark, and faster on top speed, than the saloon tested on 18 January 1963. Both cars were fitted with Laycock overdrive, and typical of the difference between them are a reduction of 13 sec. in acceleration from rest to 80 mph, and an increase of 6 mph in the direct top gear maximum.'

In the meantime, the Vitesse 1600 had also been given a revised, and much better equipped, facia and instrumental panel display. Effective from September 1963, and chassis number 15001, the Herald 1200-type facia layout was discarded. In its place was a display featuring matching speedometer and rev-counter dials, which in turn were flanked by fuel and temperature gauges, and a map pocket was added to the trim panel in the passenger's footwell.

In and around all this activity, the Vitesse was only sold as a two-door saloon or convertible. Although an estate car prototype was built in the experimental department workshops (carrying the chassis number X679) in 1961, no such derivative was put on sale by Standard-Triumph as a series-production model.

(That car, incidentally, was converted back to saloon specification in April 1962, even before the Vitesse was launched, and four years later it became the very first prototype 2-litre Vitesse saloon, later being registered FRW 898D.)

In recent years, however, a handful of Vitesse Estate cars have turned up on the 'classic' car scene, and these can be categorized in two ways. One or two of these are genuine 'private-enterprise' conversions (anyone with a good working knowledge of the architecture of Herald/Vitesse bodyshell construction could work this out), but the majority were apparently produced, to special order, as special vehicles, at the Standard-Triumph London Service Centre, which was then located in a factory on Hanger Lane, A40, not far from the Hanger Lane Underpass, and the crossing with the North Circular·Road.

It is true that once, when asked in the 1960s, Harry Webster said that the factory would produce *anything* to keep the production lines busy, but the sales departments were always adamant that there was no demand for a Vitesse Estate car, and it was never officially on offer.

All in all, the Vitesse 1600 was on sale for more than four years, in which time 31,261 cars were produced, 22,814 saloons and 8447 convertibles. In its two peak years—1963 and 1964—the Vitesse was produced at the rate of 7556 and 8322 cars respectively, which was ample to make it a very profitable machine indeed. The best-ever production month was September 1962, when 1136 Vitesses of all types were built.

In the USA, incidentally, the Vitesse was always badged as the 'Sports 6', which

The Vitesse convertible of 1962 was a smart little car which combined twin-headlamp elegance, with the practical and smooth lines of the existing convertible shell

ABOVE *From the rear, the Vitesse could be 'picked' by the canopy over its number plate (5 VC was actually Jean-Jacques Thuner's 'works' TR4 . . .), and suitable badging alongside that plate. The car also had distinctive wheel trims*

RIGHT *Three years after launch, the Vitesse nose had become very familiar to British motorists*

contrasted neatly with the contemporary 'Spitfire 4'—my colleague Richard Langworth charts its Stateside progress in a later chapter.

The original Vitesse, however, was only the first of three different models, each fiercer, and more 'sports saloon' in feel, than the last. In conjunction with the GT6, which was launched at the same time, the next derivative would be the 2-litre, and this car is surveyed in chapter 8.

Vitesse 1600

Built April 1962 to September 1966
Number built 31,261—22,814 saloons, 8447 Convertibles
Chassis numbers HB1 to HB34053 inclusive
Basic and total prices on introduction:

Saloon	£608	(Total £837)
Convertible	£649	(Total £893)

Saloon specification
Engine 6-cyl., in-line, cast-iron cylinder block and cylinder head, with four crankshaft main bearings. Bore, stroke and capacity 66.75 × 76.0 mm, 1596 cc (2.63 × 2.99 in., 97.39 cu in.). CR 8.75:1, two semi-downdraught Solex carburettors (two horizontal constant-vacuum Zenith-Stromberg carburettors from chassis no. 28061, July 1965). 70 bhp (net) at 5000 rpm. Maximum torque 92 lb ft at 2800 rpm.
Transmission Final drive ratio 4.11:1. Overall gear ratios 4.11, 5.16, 7.31, 12.06, reverse 12.06:1. Synchromesh on top, third and second gears. Optional Laycock overdrive on top and third gears, overall ratios 3.297, and 4.139:1. 16.4 mph/1000 rpm in direct top gear, 20.4 mph/1000 rpm in overdrive top.
Suspension and brakes 9.0 in. front disc brakes, 8 × 1.25 in. rear drum brakes. 5.60-13 in. tyres on 3.5 in. rim bolt-on steel disc wheels.
Dimensions Length 12 ft 9 in.; width 5 ft 0 in.; height 4 ft 4.5 in. Front track 4 ft 1 in.; rear track 4 ft 0 in. Unladen weight 2044 lb.

Convertible specification As for saloon, except for convertible body style.

Chapter 7
Herald and Vitesse in motor sport

When the original Herald was launched in 1959, Standard-Triumph's reputation in motor sport was at its peak. The 2.2-litre version of the TR3A was a formidable rally car at all levels, while the twin cam Sabrina engined TR3S models were just about to make their racing debut at Le Mans. Even the Standard Pennants had recently covered themselves with glory in the previous RAC Rally. It was almost inevitable, therefore, that a team of works Heralds would be rallied in due course.

Even so, it was asking a lot of the car even to set up creditable performances, let alone to start winning anything. There was no doubt that the 948 cc Herald was a rather under-powered car, which sold on the merits of its styling, and its technical novelty, rather than on its performance. But this did not deter management. Ever since the SC range had been put on sale, the smaller cars had been rallied, on events where the regulations, or the handicapping, was favourable. So, too, would the Herald.

From time to time, the small saloons had surprised us all, notably in the RAC Rally, which Jimmy Ray's twin-carb Standard Ten had won outright in 1955, and where Ron Gouldbourn and Tom Gold had taken second and third places in 1958. There were two excellent showings on the Tulip Rally, where target times were always subject to handicaps—in 1955 where Maurice Gatsonides finished fourth in a Standard Ten (behind two Mercedes-Benz and one Bristol!), and in 1956 where Standard Eights finished second (Wallwork), third (Hopkirk), fourth and fifth overall, behind an Austin A30—a rally for tiddlers.

So, in mid-1959, the spotlight fell on the Heralds. To make the best of a difficult job, Ken Richardson chose to use Coupés, as they had more power in standard 'showroom' form, and slightly better roadholding. However, as with the TR3A sports cars of the day, there is no evidence that the works cars were ever faster and stronger than privately-owned examples. When the author came to re-open a competitions department in 1962, he was astonished to find no surviving records of modifications made, and no evidence of power-tuning ever having been carried out by the factory's development engineers.

The first works outing for the Herald Coupé was in the Alpine Rally of June 1959. In this event, there were no fewer than four factory-backed TR3As (which beat the big Austin-Healeys for the second year in succession), so the team could only support a single Herald. It was almost an insult to the gallant little car (TL 5), that it was driven by its owner I. D. L. 'Tiny' Lewis, and Tony Nash, for 'Tiny' was the nickname of a very large rally driver indeed!

The Herald made a very promising debut. On a typically tough Alpine, where only nine cars completed the course without losing time, and gained *Coupés des Alpes*, the Herald was the ninth of these. Dudley Barker's privately entered car (WYT 393) also finished the event. The doyen of British rallying, John Gott, writing about the event in *Autosport*, thought that '"Tiny" Lewis/Tony Nash did a wonderful job to bring the new Triumph Herald through unpenalized. . . .'

For the RAC Rally, in November, where the

new organizer Jack Kemsley had promised that the event would be won 'on the road' if he had his way, a team of three Heralds was entered, to be driven by 'Tiny' Lewis, Peter Bolton and Keith Ballisat, and a further six privately-entered cars took part.

The event is chiefly remembered for the sudden snowstorm which blocked the route between Aviemore and Braemar, for the fact that dozens of cars spent hours trying to get through, and for the fact that just 15 cars (the author was in one) sped the long way round, to reach the next control within time limits.

Although the works-assisted Heralds were carrying competition numbers 125, 127 and 134 (which was 30 numbers—and, therefore, minutes on the road—behind the car in which I co-drove), none took advantage of the confusing and returning cars, to make the long-way dash. That apart, all three cars performed well, and 'Tiny' Lewis was one of only three competitors who got to every other control on time (John Wallwork's Volvo and Peter Harper's Sunbeam Rapier were the others). 'Tiny' finished 16th according to the official results, but third by any sane observer's standards.

All but the crews who had reached Braemar thought that this control should have been cancelled, but—in a way—Standard-Triumph did not mind. If the results stood as published, the TR3As won the team prize and the Heralds were second to them; if the Braemar control was cancelled, the two teams simply swapped places. Once again, Lewis had put up a fine show.

It wasn't surprising, therefore, that Ken Richardson's Allesley competitions department was stuffed full of Herald coupés before the Monte Carlo rally of January 1960. Not only two TR3As, but no fewer than six Heralds were entered, five of them being prepared at the factory. Team regulars Lewis and Ballisat took two cars, Cyril Corbishley and Eddie Hodson

The Herald's first 'team' appearance was in the RAC Rally of 1959, in which the cars finished behind the TR3As for the team prize. Here is 'Tiny' Lewis, at Prescott, driving 'TL 5', his own car, during this event

MONTE-CARLO
TRIUMPH
192

FAR LEFT *Stiffly posed for the camera, are Ken Richardson (Standard-Triumph competitions manager) in the reclining passenger seat of a Herald being prepared for rallying, and his assistant Marshall Dorr at the wheel*

LEFT *A line up of 'works' Heralds being readied for the 1960 Monte Carlo at Allesley, with Ken Richardson and Marshall Dorr looking into a coupe's engine bay*

LEFT BELOW *The Keith Ballisat/Stuart Turner 'works' Herald Coupé, at Dover, during the 1960 Monte Carlo Rally. Later this car crashed* (Courtesy Smith & Nephew Ltd.)

RIGHT *Annie Soisbault (centre), Renee Wagner (right), and the 'publicity' Cheetah, with VWK 534, before the start of the 1960 Monte Carlo Rally*

took others, while the team's star lady driver, the French girl, Annie Soisbault, took a fifth. Rob Slotemaker, the Dutchman, drove the sixth.

Annie, it was, who turned up at the start in Paris, not only with her co-driver Annie Spiers, but with a cheetah in the back seat!

The Autocar's pre-rally description told us that: 'The Heralds are running in standard mechanical form. Like all other works entries, the engines have been very carefully prepared and tuned to give maximum power on French petrol or its equivalent in octane rating. Radiator blinds, controlled from the facia panel, will be used to maintain optimum temperature. Other weather-beating equipment includes fog lamps, and a snow shield beneath the radiator.

All the cars have roof-mounted, swivelling spot lamps, and reversing lights. Apart from the addition of a Halda Speed Pilot, two chronostop watches and extra switches, the facia is normal . . . the driving seat of each Herald is a production model, but the angle of the back rest of the navigator's seat can be adjusted by altering the position of two small chains, and a thickly padded headrest is also fitted. The luggage locker carries extra fuel, oil and water in addition to two spare wheels.

Like other British works entries, the Triumphs will be using the latest pattern Dunlop Duraband tyres fitted with tungsten-steel studs. . . .'

Yet, in spite of all that effort, the factory had little to show for their expensive efforts, even though the indefatigable 'Tiny' Lewis was one of only nine crews to reach Monte Carlo, before the final test, without road penalties. Ballisat (with co-driver Stuart Turner, later to become competitions supremo at BMC, and more recently at Ford) crashed his car, while Slotemaker holed a radiator against a rock in the road, on the final stages.

Three of the crews—Lewis, Corbishley and Annie Soisbault—qualified to tackle the final regularity test, which was completely dominated by the Mercedes-Benz team, and Corbishley managed to finish 25th, and third in his capacity class. The unfortunate 'Tiny', however, suffered from an electrical failure in his Herald's wiring loom, and finished near the back of the field.

Things could only get better, after that outing, and in the Tulip rally, fortunately they did. Driving YRW 267 'Tiny' Lewis and Tony Nash won their class, with Geoff Mabbs close behind him in second place. All the other team regulars were in TR3As.

Nevertheless, it was rapidly becoming clear that the Herald was no longer competitive, and Richardson was depressed by the pace of the two-stroke DKWs and Saabs, and the promise of the new front-wheel-drive Minis, all of which were in the same capacity group. After the summer of 1960, in any case, Standard-

ABOVE *Cyril Corbishley and Peter Roberts, on ice covered roads in the French Alps, during the 1960 Monte*

RIGHT *'Tiny' Lewis and Tony Nash, Herald YRW 268, at St Pierre de Chartreuse, near Chambéry in the Monte Carlo Rally*

Triumph's competitions activity was rapidly run down as a financial crisis set in, and a full team of Heralds never appeared again.

'Tiny' was nevertheless retained to drive one of the cars, against fearful odds. In the Alpine of 1960, he finished, but well out of the awards, though in the RAC Rally, at the end of the year, in which special stages were used for the first time on a British rally, he won his class (using 8166 DU, works-loaned rather than works-entered), against an opposition which included the works Ford Anglia 105Es, and no fewer than 14 other Heralds!

In the Monte, also the year in which special stages were used for the first time, 'Tiny' could finish no higher than 25th overall, though he was consoled with the prize for the best performance by a Glasgow starter, the Royal Scottish Automobile Club trophy.

The Herald's swansong, however, was also its finest hour, and came in the Tulip rally of 1961. The Tulip, I remind the reader, was an event riddled with handicapping, on this occasion involving a class improvement system. In other words, the car which was outstandingly better than its class rivals would finish higher than a car in another class, which had only won it narrowly.

As usual, only 'Tiny' Lewis turned up in a factory-provided Herald—YRW 266, this time—but he was also rivalled by private owner Geoff Mabbs, in a car registered 111 LHW. Lewis and Mabbs, both Bristolians, were firm friends, but they were both rivals, as well. From

the start of the event, they fought hard, mile by mile, for the lead.

The rally, which started and finished at Noordwijk aan Zee, in Holland, followed its usual course, with fairly easy road sections leading down to Monte Carlo, an overnight halt in the Principality, and a long run back. Along the way there were several special stages and hillclimbs, the results always being calculated in terms of class percentage performance.

Although 'Tiny' was slightly faster than Mabbs, there was little in it, all the way south, until 'Tiny' lost two minutes on an earlier section when the throttle linkage parted. At half distance, therefore, Skogh's Saab led the event, on 94.13 per cent, with Walter's Porsche second, Bohringer's Mercedes-Benz saloon third, and Geoff Mabbs fourth, on 95.93 per cent. Lewis was not in the top 15, actually lying 20th.

All the way back to Holland, the battle between the two Heralds continued, with little showing up between them. Near the end, there was plenty of time for the two crews to think, and for the two experienced co-drivers (Leslie Griffiths with Mabbs, David Stone with Lewis) to do a few sums.

And so it was decided. To the consternation of everyone—not least the unlucky Walter, from Germany, who was always likely to bring his Porsche Carrera to victory—the two Heralds reached Noordwijk aan Zee, but only one of them actually clocked in at the finish! Lewis had seen a loophole in the handicapping rules, realized that if he 'retired' his car, then Mabbs' class performance would be outstandingly good, and promptly withdrew the works-loaned car.

It was amazing. At a stroke, Mabbs' penalty dropped to 94.35 per cent, which was a full percentage point better than that of the

YRW 269

Porsche, and he gained a much-discussed outright victory. (He also won his capacity class, naturally, but Standard-Triumph didn't need to worry about advertising that.) The irony of it all was that the 948 cc Herald which won its only international rally had already been made obsolete, for the Herald 1200 had been launched three weeks earlier. . . .

There was nothing wrong with 'Tiny' Lewis' car, of course, for it turned up at the finish, looking hale and hearty, without handing in its road book or time cards. However, as Gregor Grant, *Autosport*'s editor, said in his report:

'Mabbs' engine was stripped down by the organizers and found to be perfectly standard. There was, of course, criticism of Lewis' action, but in the circumstances it is difficult to see how he could have done otherwise.'

And that, as far as the Herald was concerned, was that, for by May 1961 Leyland had taken over Standard-Triumph, the competitions department was completely bound up in preparing the TRS prototypes for the Le Mans 24 Hours race, and money was short. It would be more than a year before the factory once again became interested in rallying a car of the Herald family.

Vitesse in rallying

After the Le Mans 24 Hours race in June 1961, Ken Richardson's competitions department was immediately closed down, and there was then a six-month gap before Harry Webster instructed the author to set up a new department, this time based in the Fletchamstead North building of the Canley site, where all design and development was taking place. To make way for a team of new TR4 sports cars, the tractor project was moved out.

In that short time, a great deal had been happening in the world of international rallying, which effectively made the Herald obsolete as a competition car. Apart from the trend towards using loose-surface special stages in British events (the RAC rally of 1961 opened those particular floodgates . . .), there had been the arrival of the Mini-Cooper at BMC. This tiny one-litre car was the first of the 'homologation specials', and it was quite clear that the Herald, even the Herald 1200, would not be competitive again.

In the meantime, the Vitesse arrived on the scene, and in my capacity as competitions secretary, I used the white-and-black prototype, registered 407 VC, as a service/chase car on the Alpine rally in June. It told me, and my passenger Mick Moore, two things—that if the suspension was suitably set up then the handling would be fine for competitions, and that it needed a lot more power to be competitive.

(The disturbing feature of this trip was that the Triumph team stayed in the same pre-start hotel, near Marseilles, on the French Riviera, as the Ford works team, and during the inevitable chat and 'bull' sessions we not only learned of the imminent arrival of the Cortina, but of the existence of the car later to become known as the Lotus-Cortina.

One thing seemed certain—that although the principal competition in 1962 came from the Sunbeam Rapier, the Citroen DS19 and the Volvo 122S, in 1963 there would be altogether quicker cars on the scene.)

The very first job taken on by the newly-opened competitions department in February 1962 was to build a Herald 1200 saloon for use in the East African Safari. Not a full-blown works entry, however, but prepared for Bob Halmi of New York to drive (his co-drivers were M. Smith and M. Singh). This 1200 started well, but failed to finish, in a class dominated by VW Beetles.

By the autumn of 1962, however, management wanted to try out a Vitesse, at least, for the sales department were much more enthusiastic about the idea of sending works saloons on events, than works sports cars. It was a simple question of sales potential—for TR4 sales in Europe were limited, and American buyers were not really influenced by competition results over in Europe.

LEFT ABOVE *Ken Richardson (left) and 'Tiny' Lewis, planning a rally route, in Herald days*

LEFT *The old firm – 'Tiny' Lewis and Tony Nash, this time in YRW 269, in the Alpine Rally of 1960*

121

121

For the RAC rally of November 1962, therefore, it was decided to prepare 407 VC to compete. The TR4 team, and the regular drivers, were already committed, so the drive was offered to a young man called Vic Elford, who had once been David Seigle-Morris' co-driver, who had already been racing Mini-Minors, and who was now proving his abilities in a DKW in British events. For this event Elford's co-driver was to be Mike Butler, and the car was entered in the Appendix J Group 3 'Grand Touring' category, running, among other things, with a triple-SU 1.6-litre engine, producing more than 95 bhp (the records have not been preserved, however), and with twin nine-gallon fuel tanks. Other items of equipment, apart from full undershielding to protect the car's vitals, included wide-rim wheels, as specified for the Herald Courier van, special front seats, and a gutted interior.

Elford and the Vitesse started very well, and very fast, looking stable and nimble on the forestry stages, but before half distance the standard Vitesse gearbox began to give trouble. It was asking a lot for this unit to transmit 95 bhp, and a lot more torque than standard (let's not forget that the gearbox casing was still that of the 948 cc Herald, and there really wasn't much room inside for stronger gears), and in the end the mechanics, led by Ray Henderson, had to attempt a change.

In those days, no-one had worked out the way to provide quick-change gearboxes (the ten minute changes found on late-1970s Escorts and Chevettes were a long way ahead!), so the change had to be done by conventional means, in a Triumph dealer's premises in Penrith, during the Lake District loop. The seats had to come out, followed by the gearbox tunnel moulding (there were no carpets), and it took

BOTH LEFT *Coming . . . . and going, on his way to a famous victory, is Geoff Mabbs, partnered by Leslie Griffiths. Following the tactical withdrawal of 'Tiny' Lewis from the Tulip Rally of 1961, Mabbs won the event outright*

BELOW . . . *and this was how the car was displayed at Canley in the following week*

well over 90 minutes to get the job done, after which the car was outside time limits.

That year, incidentally, the 1.6-litre GT class was won by a 1-litre Mini-Cooper (driven by Rauno Aaltonen), and the best 'standard' 1.6-litre car was 'Tiny' Lewis' Sunbeam Rapier, which finished fourth overall. Gregor Grant of *Autosport*, at least, was very kind to the Vitesse in his review of the event:

'Most impressive was the six-cylinder Vitesse driven by Vic Elford and Mike Butler, and its incredible lock was of immense advantage on the countless hairpins of the special stages.'

The lessons of this outing were several, and various. The good news was that the car was clearly strong enough, and well-balanced enough, to face up to more international rallying, but it was still not competitive, even with a modified engine, and it had a weak transmission (the team had always known about this).

For 1963, however, it was decided to build a complete team of Vitesses, and for the start of the season enter three of them for the Monte Carlo rally. Accordingly four powder blue saloons arrived in the department in December 1962, for which the easy-to-remember registration numbers 6001 VC/6002 VC/6003 VC/6004 VC were allocated.

For the Monte, 'old nail', 407 VC, was used for reconnaissance, 6004 VC was the team spare, used by the author as a 'chase car' during the event, while the other three were allocated to John Sprinzel/Sam Actman, Mike Sutcliffe/Roy Fidler and Vic Elford/Mike Butler.

This time the cars were all basically standard, except that an experimental Lockheed anti-lock braking system was fitted to all of them, at Lockheed's suggestion. The anti-lock relied on a rotating sensor, which was belt driven from a pulley clamped between the propeller shaft and the final drive flange; sudden changes in rotating speed resulted in a servo cutting off brake fluid pressure to the rear drums, and stopping lock-up. Front discs could be, and still were, locked up under extreme pedal pressure.

Because the regulations allowed it, all cars were fitted with completely non-standard instrument panels, which incorporated rev counters ahead of the drivers' eyes, flanked by auxiliary instruments (of TR4 type), while the TR4 style speedometer was ahead of the co-driver's eyes, along with an accurate clock, a spare 'panic button' for the air horns, and other navigational equipment. There were Microcell front seats (that for the co-driver could be reclined), overdrive was fitted to all cars, and the handbrake was converted to fly-off operation.

Two of the cars—Sutcliffe's and Elford's—were entered in Group 2, and fitted with Mangoletsi-modified cylinder heads and camshaft profiles, while Sprinzel's car was standard. All had lowered rear suspension, wide-rim wheels, and adjustable Armstrong dampers all round.

The lighting system was interesting—the normal four headlamps were retained, there was a single, high-mounted, centre spot lamp on the nose of the bonnet, and twin back-mounting fog lamps, low down, on each side of the numberplate position. Plus, need I say, a large (and illegally bright!) reverse lamp. . . .

For recognition purposes, each of the cars had a slightly different colour scheme—Sprinzel's car having dark blue 'spears' along the flanks and across the nose, Sutcliffe's had white 'spears', while Elford's car was pure powder blue.

Before the start of the event, *Motor* were very encouraging: '. . . should the snow lie round about, deep and crisp if not exactly even, then the slim Vitesse with its great traction might well spring the surprise of the rally.' The team themselves, however, were under no illusions, for by this time the shortcomings of the six-cylinder engine's cylinder head and breathing were well-known, as was the capability of the transmission—all that could be hoped was that the versatility of the drivers, particularly Vic Elford, already seen as one of Britain's coming Superstars, would help produce a result.

In the event, the 1963 Monte was one of the most wintry on record, and it was something of a miracle that all three Vitesses arrived at the finish, undamaged. All started from Paris, and

With this sort of specification (about 100 bhp for a 1964 Spitfire race car!), how fast might a Herald rally car have been?

the story of this start-point is summarized in the statistics—80 starters, 28 finishers! Only eight cars reached Monte Carlo without road penalty, one of them being the remarkable Mr Elford. It was a rally dominated by front-wheel-drive cars (eight of the top ten, including the winner, Erik Carlsson's Saab), and the best of the 1.6-litre saloons was Peter Harper's works Sunbeam Rapier, whose total penalty time on the six special stages was 145 min. 40 sec. and his total rally penalty 3335.52. He finished 17th overall. Vic Elford's total stage penalty was 144 min. 05 sec., but his rally penalty was 3411.765, the reason being that as a Group 2 car he incurred a bigger 'handicapping' factor. The Rapier, of course, though very well-specified, was in Group One.

Even so, there were no awards, and a class third, and 24th overall, was not good enough for anyone. Back at the factory, the post-mortem was easy enough to perform. Given time, and development money (both were in short supply) the Vitesse could certainly be made better than the existing opposition—*if* it could be given a stronger transmission. The team themselves were pessimistic—during the Monte Carlo Rally the Lotus-Cortina had been unveiled, with 105 bhp (and a twin-cam engine) in only a standard tune, and with 140–150 bhp promised for full-house competition use.

There was no point, it was suggested, in throwing money at the evolution of the Vitesse (and competition parts had to be made available in numbers, for homologation to be possible) if it could still not match and beat the Ford. So that was that, and the cars were relegated to use as test and service machines.

Or so it seemed at the time. Later in the

spring, however, Vic Elford (who, in his then profession as a salesman for life assurance, had developed a very persuasive tongue), managed to get approval for his Monte car (6003 VC) to be re-prepared, in a triple-SU condition, to tackle the first-ever Manx Trophy Rally in the Isle of Man. Like all the later Manx rallies, it was a speed event from start to finish.

Autocar's report tells the story: 'Vic Elford's Vitesse, running as No. 1, carried a substitute local navigator who had already memorized the complicated route, and arrived at control 16 without reference to the Ordnance Survey map. Unfortunately the differential failed at this point and the first of the favourites was out.' He had, in fact, been leading the event, but the differential failure was complete, and catastrophic. The same old trouble had struck again.

Elford, however, was a persistent rally driver, as many a team manager has discovered since then. Faced with the idea of taking a TR4 around the Jugoslavian and Bulgarian 'roads', in Spa-Sofia-Liège in September, he asked for a much-modified Vitesse instead. This was refused. He asked again, and this time the team manager (the author) referred the request to Harry Webster. It was refused yet again. Nothing daunted, Elford then approached Donald Stokes in London, pleaded a very eloquent case, and finally got his way!

In a blazing hurry, and with no chance to carry out any testing, or development, 6003 VC was gutted, and completely rebuilt as a no-holds-barred special, for the rules of the Liège positively encouraged this. This was what went into it:

A 1998 cc Triumph 2000-type engine, with triple SUs and fabricated manifolds (as seen earlier on 407 VC), producing about 110 bhp, and lots of torque;

TR4 clutch, gearbox, and overdrive;

Triumph 2000/TR4A type of final drive unit (the 2000 was due to be revealed about six weeks after the rally, so supplies were already available);

Beefed up propeller shaft, and rear drive shafts;

Unique bonnet panels, with extra air intake on the top, larger and deeper radiator cut-outs, single seven-inch headlamps, and five auxiliary driving lamps;

A larger cooling radiator, I believe of TR4 type but modified.

This was finished off, quite literally, on the boat on the way over the channel, and in a garage in Liège before the start, but it was as good, and as fast, as it was ever likely to be, when the flag dropped.

In those days, the phenomenal, final years of the rally, the Liège started with a long, easy, run down to the Jugoslavian border, an equally long run down to Bulgaria, and an hour's rest at Sofia, followed by a fast, and amazingly rough, scramble back through Skopje, Pec, Titograd, Split, and Novi, to Italy, where a further night's pass-storming remained—all this before the long run back towards Belgium started!

For this event Elford took Terry Hunter, which effectively made it two drivers in the team, and there was no doubt that *this* Vitesse was both fast and strong enough to challenge for the lead. And so it did. After a trouble-free run to Sofia, and restarting at its competition number of 34, Elford began carving his way up towards the lead. By the time he reached Split, about half way through the 24-hour long 'breaker's-yard' section, he was up in third or fourth place—the only cars performing better being Bohringer's Mercedes-Benz 230SL, which eventually won the event, Erik Carlsson's Saab, and one or other of the Austin-Healey 3000s, the fastest being driven by Rauno Aaltonen.

Then, quite suddenly, the Vitesse caught fire, near Bribir, and the drivers were lucky to get out without injury. The car's extinguisher could not cope, and the machine burned out, taking three hours to do so. The factory never discovered why, even though the wreckage was eventually returned to Coventry for inspection, though it was always suspected that a petrol pipe had broken, and sprayed fuel over the hot engine.

Rumours that it was crashed first were untrue, as the wreckage confirmed, for every panel was still straight, even though the whole car was gutted by the fire.

By this time the competitions department

The 'works' Vitesses only appeared as a full team on one occasion, at Monte Carlo in 1963, when this car was driven by Mike Sutcliffe and Roy Fidler. A sister car, driven by Vic Elford, finished third in its class

had more ambitious projects in mind—which included racing Spitfires at Le Mans, and rallying the big 2000s in rough road events—so the Liège fire spelt the absolute end of the Vitesse competitions programme, at least as far as the factory was concerned.

It is worth mentioning, by the way, that a virtually standard Vitesse 1600 was raced in *The Motor* six-hour race at Brands Hatch in October 1962, where it was driven by John Sprinzel and Neil Dangerfield. However, this was not a works entry, for it had been prepared by Syd Hurrell's tuning concern, and it struck trouble right at the beginning of the event (with a punctured carburettor float chamber), and did not figure in the results.

An author is allowed to indulge, just a little, in an 'if only' exercise on such occasions.

The very special 2-litre Vitesse prototype, as driven by Vic Elford and Terry Hunter (driving at this moment) in the Spa-Sofia-Liège marathon. It had a 1998 cc six-cylinder engine, a TR4 gearbox, a TR4A type differential, and a very distinctive front end style. When well placed, it was burnt out by an accidental under-bonnet fire, thought to be due to leaking fuel

Knowing what happened to the development of the Spitfires in later years, and knowing how the six-cylinder engines themselves were improved during the mid-1960s, it is interesting, though fruitless, to speculate how competitive a Vitesse might have been with a deep-breathing engine, and a strong transmission. Perhaps even better as a 2-litre, with fuel injection like the 2.5PI, rather than as a 1.6-litre car, a Vitesse might have become a tremendously fast rallying projectile. But in that case, would the rallying 2.5PIs ever have been developed at all?

Chapter 8
Vitesse 2-litre: some even better than others

Standard-Triumph made a great occasion of the launch of the new GT6 Coupé, in October 1966, so much so that many press men almost missed the arrival of the Vitesse 2-litre, which shared most of the pretty little Coupé's mechanical components. Yet in terms of numbers built and sold, the Vitesse was still a very important car.

It was one of those cars that everyone seemed to think would inevitably appear. After all, even the most amateur 'product-planner' could see that the larger, 1998 cc, version of the six-cylinder engine would easily fit under the Vitesse's bonnet, though not many of them could have realized just how much work would be needed to make the transmission behind that engine stay in one piece!

Until the 1970s, in any case, no car maker ever seemed to produce a new model which was smaller, slower, and less well-equipped than its predecessor. It was all a matter of 'prestige', and so-called progress. Ever since motoring had begun, it seemed, the *next* car had to have more power, more performance, and better equipment—all of which would make it easier for the advertising staff to boast about the new generation.

In the 1960s, in fact, Standard-Triumph went in for a positive orgy of uprating, and up-grading the engines for their cars. The Herald, as we shall see, went up from 948 cc to 1296 cc, the TR from 1991 cc to 2498 cc, and the new Stag from 2498 cc to 2998 cc (even before it was launched).

The Vitesse was to be no exception. It lasted just over four years in its original 1596 cc form, before giving way to the new 2-litre model. The new derivative, incidentally, would be one of the most controversial yet produced by the company.

Behind the scenes, incidentally, there never seemed to be much drama, or difficulty, about fitting the enlarged engine to the Herald/Vitesse, and Spitfire/GT6 chassis frames. Physically, of course, it was no problem, and after all the very first six-cylinder engined prototype—produced for Harry Webster at the end of 1959—had had a 2-litre engine installed.

There were two obvious reasons for producing the 2-litre Vitesse. One, quite clearly, was that it would make the car mechanically very similar to the GT6, if not quite as fast. The other was that the Vitesse 1600 had never had as much performance as some of its clientele wished, and it needed to be improved.

As I have already mentioned in an earlier chapter, time and the opposition caught up rapidly with the Vitesse 1600. Other manufacturers, notably Ford, produced quicker and more economical 1.5/1.6-litre sports saloons, such that the Vitesse began to struggle to keep its market share. Not only that, but Leyland management repeatedly asked for passenger cars which would pull well from low engine speeds, for they did not want their customers to have to work away at the gear lever to get good traffic performance out of their cars. One way to achieve this, on any car, is to use a larger engine which develops its torque lower down the rev range.

First thoughts about installing the larger engine into the Vitesse surfaced in Engineering in 1963, when it immediately became apparent that the existing close-ratio Vitesse gearbox could not handle the extra torque developed by the 1998 cc unit. It was also embarrassingly clear that the final drive unit would not stand the strain either. Nor was that merely the ultra-cautious design engineers worrying too much; the very first Spitfire rally cars, which produced about 100 bhp, though less torque than the proposed 2-litre Vitesse, used close-ratio (unsynchronized first gear) Vitesse gearboxes, and inflicted terrible punishment on them.

The secret to developing new 2-litre Vitesse *and* GT6 models, therefore, was to produce a strong enough transmission to go behind the engine. The expensive way out, of course, would have been to fit the Triumph 2000/TR4A type of gearbox and final drive components, but this was not practical. Both were physically larger, heavier, *and* more expensive than the Vitesse units.

(Producing Vic Elford's Spa-Sofia-Liège 'special' of 1963 had proved all this, so it was not even necessary to build another prototype!)

For the new Vitesse and GT6 cars, therefore (and with an eye to adopting them on other models, in due course), it was decided to develop new and stronger derivatives of the existing gearbox and back axle. It was a typical fast, resourceful, and pragmatic Standard-Triumph solution, the sort for which Harry Webster, and George Jones (his transmissions

RIGHT *Because the 2-litre engine was physically the same size as the superseded 1.6-litre unit, it fitted comfortably under the Vitesse's bonnet. The slim air-cleaner tucked neatly between the carbs, and the splash guards inboard of the front suspension towers*

BELOW *The powerhouse of the Vitesse 2-litre model (and GT6) was this efficient, 95 bhp, 1998 cc engine, much more torquey than the 1.6-litre unit it replaced. Behind it, of course, was the all-synchromesh transmission, first used in prototype form in the 'works' Spitfire rally cars*

specialist, at the time) were already noted.

Without spending a small fortune on new machine tools and fixtures, a new and sturdy all-synchromesh gearbox was produced, which still retained the same basic dimensions as the existing Herald/Vitesse box, and took up very little extra space. Not only did it have synchromesh on all forward gears (like the TR4/Triumph 2000 gearbox, though this was an entirely different, and rather larger, component), but it was a much sturdier design, capable of handling a lot more torque.

Although it was never publicly announced at the time, the new all-synchromesh gearbox found very valuable use in the works Spitfire rally programme of 1964 to 1966. The first event tackled by the powder-blue Spitfires was the Alpine rally of June 1964, when they were equipped with close-ratio Vitesse 1600-type gearboxes. Experience in the event showed that the very 'peaky' four-cylinder engines needed the use of first gear frequently, particularly in the mountains.

On returning from the event, the drivers asked if anything could be done, and must have been astonished to be offered all-synchromesh gears for their next outing! Even by Webster standards, it was a very quick turn around—the Alpine was in June, the post-mortem in July, and all four Spitfires for the Tour de France were equipped with all-synchromesh boxes!

Did I hear a mention of homologation? Well, the fact was that this box was never homologated, but then Standard-Triumph were only following the lead of their British and European rivals in this respect. . . .

For the record, here are the ratios of the 'new' and 'old' Vitesse gearboxes:

2-litre/GT6:	1.00, 1.25, 1.78, 2.65, reverse 3.10:1
1600:	1.00, 1.25, 1.78, 2.94*, reverse 2.94:1

*Unsynchronized first gear ratio

As before, an overdrive was to be optional equipment, both on the Vitesse and the GT6.

The chassis-mounted differential, similarly, looked familiar, but was much changed. As I said in my original *Autocar* description in 1966:

'. . . the differential is a new design. Changes have been made to accept the new high ratio, with 36 teeth on the crown wheel and 11 on the pinion; its output flanges are bigger and stronger than before, with 9/16 in. bolts attaching the half-shafts.'

In the next decade, in fact, this beefed-up differential was to be made with 3.27, 3.63, and 3.89:1 ratios—for the first of the Vitesse two-litre cars the 3.89:1 ratio was used, with or without overdrive being specified.

The rest of the mechanical changes were straightforward, and logical. As fitted to the latest Vitesse, and the GT6, the 1998 cc engine produced 95 bhp (net) at 5000 rpm, with the aid of twin horizontal Zenith-Stromberg 150CD carburettors, and a 9.5:1 compression ratio. (In the near-equivalent Triumph 2000, the CR was 9.0:1, and peak power was 90 bhp.)

There was a complex new cooling system layout, and the previous remote header tank was no longer fitted. The new radiator was more squat, and had its filler cap on an upwards extension, tucked just underneath the bonnet panel. The engine's inlet manifold was water heated, and there was an expansion bottle connected to the overflow pipe.

Behind the engine was a new Borg & Beck diaphragm spring clutch, of 8.5 in. diameter.

Chassis changes included the use of wider wheel rims (the 4.5 in. variety, as already found on the Courier van), larger front discs of 9.7 in. diameter, bigger calipers, and an increased

RIGHT *The only way to 'pick' a Vitesse 2-litre from the 1600 was by looking carefully for the badges on the grille, and the flanks just ahead of the doors, plus a different boot badge*

RIGHT BELOW *No excuse for not knowing what model had just passed you – if, that is, you had time to read the badge before the car disappeared into the distance!*

BELOW *The Vitesse 2-litre engine bay was neatly packaged, but not crowded*

FVC 227D

FVC 227D
Vitesse
2
LITRE

LEFT *The secret of the improved handling, in the Vitesse 2-litre Mk 2, was in the revised rear suspension geometry. Not quite obvious here is the new lower wishbone, though the big rubber 'doughnut' C/V joint in the drive shaft is clear, as is the position of the hydraulic lever arm dampers, on new brackets behind the main cross 'bridge'. Note, also, the use of radial ply tyres, and the widened (TR5-type) cylinder head in the 104 bhp engine . . .*

BELOW . . . *while this technical 'exploded' drawing should make the layout of the 'lower-wishbone' rear suspension easier to understand. Compared with the early 2-litre, the engineering was more complex, but the result was certainly worth the effort*

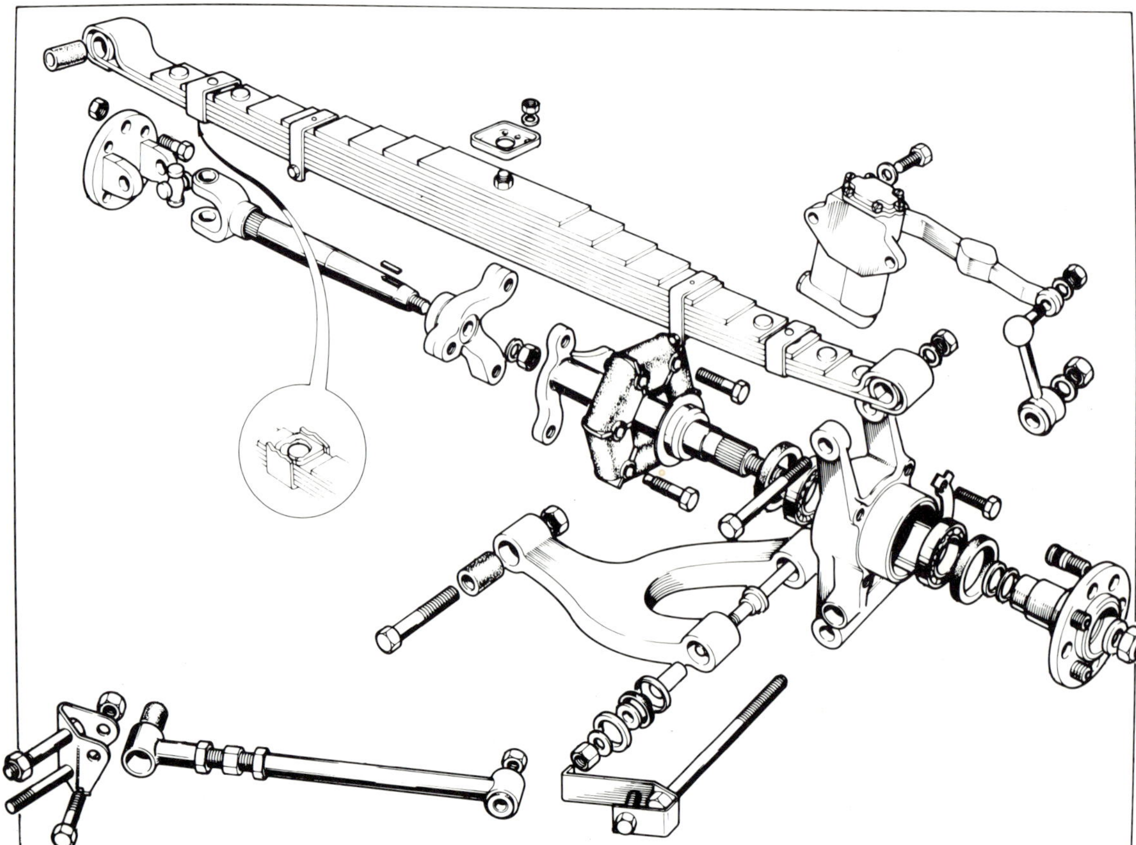

swept area. Cross-ply tyres, however, were still fitted, but the TR4 spring-spoke steering wheel was now specified.

Re-styling changes were few. Apart from the 2-litre badges on the front grille, the sides of the bonnet above the catches, and on the boot lid, there was a reverse lamp automatically illuminated when the gear lever was moved into the reverse slot, while the seats had been redesigned. As with the 1600, only two-door saloon, or convertible, body styles were offered.

Perhaps the appeal of the new car was ideally summed up by the motoring writer, Gordon Wilkins, in his regular *Standard-Triumph Review* column:

'To me the Vitesse has been a disappointing car in its 1½-litre form. It never seemed to achieve the top-gear performance one hoped for from a six-cylinder engine in a light car. Nor did it provide an adequate recompense for the effort of threshing up and down through four gears and two overdrive gears. The two-litre engine has changed all that. The Vitesse has really come to life. Driving with a light load one can leave most of the other traffic behind simply by starting in second, making a quick rush up to 40, then changing straight into top for a powerful surge of acceleration up to 90 or whatever speed the law allows. . . .'

It was, by any standards, a much quicker car than the 1600 which it displayed. When *Autocar* tested GWK 890D in the spring of 1967—a saloon, fitted with the optional (for £58.34) overdrive—they clocked a 95 mph top speed, and 0–60 mph in 12.6 sec., with overall fuel consumption of 26.1 mpg. One comment in the text was: 'Compared with a Herald we have been driving recently, the Vitesse feels like a dragster. . . .'

By this time, however, testers were beginning to show real disquiet about the unmodified swing-axle rear suspension:

'With all the power, the tail of the car can be made to slide wide on dry roads, and needs a lot of watching on wet ones. Even at 30 mph on quite gradual bends, too wide a throttle in second gear can flick the rear wheels sideways quite suddenly, and a full understanding of the car is essential for safety . . . if the driver lifts off the throttle on entering a bend, there is weight transfer forwards which suddenly reduces the rear wheel cornering power, and can make the tail flick out alarmingly. . . .'

A look at other road tests published of this car, and of the original GT6, shows that there was concerted technical press criticism of the swing axle rear suspension. However, both Harry Webster and John Lloyd have both stated, quite adamantly, that there was little adverse reaction from the general public:

'I think Harry knew what we were faced with, at the back end,' John Lloyd reminisces, 'and I think he knew that with an altered suspension we would be without one of the car's known weaknesses. So we worked up the new system on the Vitesse first—that was the forerunner, and we applied it to the GT6 later. There was never any (development) trouble with that back end at all, no whirling speed troubles, nothing.'

Although later events showed that the simple swing-spring type of independent rear suspension, which had been developed at Banner Lane during 1959, it was never applied to the Vitesse. Instead, the engineers produced a radically new geometry, which is now always known as the 'lower-wishbone' system.

Although now, by current standards, it looks crude, and something of a lash-up, it was a brilliant stroke of improvisation. Compared with the first layout, the original chassis frame was retained, as was the differential, and the transverse leaf spring bolted down to it. New vertical links were provided to support the wheel hubs, and a 'reverse' type of lower wishbone was then tied between the bottom of this link, and new brackets on the chassis side-member.

Because the effective length of the drive shafts would no longer be fixed, it was necessary to provide some 'plunge'. Splines would be expensive (and were already giving lots of trouble on the 2000 and TR4A/5 models), so a rubber 'doughnut' universal joint, as used at the front of the Triumph 1300, was used. These joints had a very limited fatigue life at first, and tended to split across the bolt holes, but development cured that one.

The suspension layout was completed by the relocation of dampers—still telescopic, but more upright, for the GT6, but hydraulic lever arm type for the Vitesse, and mounted behind the line of the drive shafts, alongside the rear cross-member 'bridge'.

It was a remarkably effective modification, made in a very restricted space, and quite transformed the roadholding and stability of any car to which it was fitted, so Standard-Triumph hastened to bring it into production. All of which explains why the original 2-litre Vitesse was only built from September 1966 to September 1968—there being approximately 12,000 produced in those two years.

The new derivative, logically named Vitesse 2-litre Mk 2, was launched in October 1968, but was a much more comprehensively redesigned package than expected. Up front, the engine was given the latest type of cylinder head, which had an altogether wider cross section, and more efficient breathing. This, allied to a more ambitious camshaft profile, gave the engine 104 bhp (net) at 5300 rpm; the GT6 became Mk 2 at the same time, with the same mechanical changes.

Radial ply tyres, of 155SR-13 in. section, had already been standard for some time, and were now united with the new rear suspension. This, incidentally, had a 6.3 in. high roll centre, instead of 12.75 in. on the old swing axle system, the rear spring had 11 slim leaves rather than seven thicker ones, and a rate of 93 lb in. instead of 84 lb/in. The net result was 15 per cent stiffer suspension, and much better and more predictable roadholding.

The Mk 2, incidentally, was the quickest Vitesse yet, as *Autocar*'s figures—a 101 mph top speed, 0–60 mph in 11.9 sec., and sparkling acceleration in each gear, confirmed. Since this magazine had been so rude about the original 2-litre, it is worth noting that they thought there was: 'Much better handling and roadholding', which made all the effort worthwhile.

The Vitesse 2-litre Mk 2 had a distinctive slatted grille style (though the basic sheet metal was not changed), pseudo-Rostyle wheel trims, and a new 'Vitesse' badge on the nose of the bonnet . . .

The Mk 2, incidentally, had been made distinctive, externally, by the use of a new front grille, a ceramic panel across the boot lid recess, and new badging, plus simulated magnesium alloy wheel trims. Internally, the facia had been restyled, rather in the same way as the Herald 13/60 (described in the next chapter), with a recessed centre panel for the switches. In addition, the auxiliary instruments had now been placed outboard of the speedometer (on the left, for a right-hand drive car), and the rev-counter (right). As before the Vitesse was still significantly the cheapest six-cylinder engined car on sale in the UK.

By this time, however, the Vitesse had become something of a forgotten model in the Triumph range. It had come to the end of its sensible development potential (of course it would have been possible to fit the larger 2498 cc engine, either with twin carbs, or even with Lucas fuel injection! but this was never seriously considered), and was coasting along, well-promoted in advertising, but no longer being improved.

As early as 1966, Standard-Triumph had begun to look for ways of replacing the Vitesse, and at that stage the concept of a rear-wheel-drive conversion to the 1300's bodyshell, with the brand new slant-four, overhead-camshaft 'Saab' engine, was being considered. That car, with a choice of 1500 or 1709 cc engines, might have been ready for 1969, if needed, and was tentatively called 'the new Vitesse' by the directors. As we now know, this project was delayed, further delayed, and eventually appeared at the beginning of 1972 as the 1854 cc Dolomite.

After 1967, therefore, it is interesting to see the way that Vitesse sales slowly declined. In 1967 (and in spite of criticism of the rear suspension) 6994 2-litres were built, but this fell to 4697 in 1968, 3961 in 1969, and 1981 in 1970. By the beginning of 1971, only 20 to 30 Vitesses were being built every week, and the last of the

. . . while at the rear there was brightwork across the tail recess

saloons was finished in mid March, after which a further 98 convertibles followed. The last Vitesse of all was built in the week ending 17 May 1971; Herald 13/60 assembly ceased at the same time. Only 471 were built in 1971 calendar year. It was no coincidence that volume production of Dolomites began a matter of weeks later.

How to sum up the 2-litre Vitesse, particularly in Mk 2 form? A good car, certainly, and in the right hands, fast and exciting to drive. In fairness, though, by 1971 it was lagging well behind the times, as far as its competitors were concerned. There was not enough room inside the cabin, there was no four-door option, nor an automatic, and the ride was beginning to look harsh. The particular merits of the separate chassis frame/built-up body were long forgotten, and the taxi-like turning circle was no longer needed by many people.

Yet it *must* have been a profitable project to Standard-Triumph, for no fewer than 19,951 2-litres were produced in five years, from a very small capital tooling investment. Along with the 13/60, which I survey in the next chapter, it successfully prolonged the life of the family for a number of years.

RIGHT *The 2-litre Mk 2 Convertible was very popular, and was on sale right to the end, in 1971*

ABOVE *Under that purposeful bonnet is a potential 104 bhp, which could give the Vitesse 2-litre Mk 2 a 100 mph top speed*

Facts and figures: Vitesse 2-litre

General specification

Facts and figures: Vitesse 2-litre
General specification

Built September 1966 to September 1968
Number built 10,830—7328 saloons, 3502 Convertibles
Chassis numbers HC1 to HC12079 inclusive
Basic and total price on introduction:

Saloon	£681	(Total £839)
Convertible	£717	(Total £883)

Saloon specification
Engine 6-cyl., in-line, cast-iron cylinder block and cylinder head, with four crankshaft main bearings. Bore, stroke and capacity 74.7 × 76.0 mm, 1998 cc (2.94 × 2.99 in., 122 cu in.). CR 9.5:1. Two horizontal constant-vacuum Zenith-Stromberg carburettors. 95 bhp (net) at 5000 rpm. Maximum torque 117 lb ft at 3000 rpm.
Transmission Final drive ratio 3.89:1. Overall gear ratios 3.89, 4.86, 6.92, 10.30, reverse 12.06:1. Synchromesh on all forward gears. Optional Laycock overdrive on top and third gears, overall ratios 3.11, and 3.93:1. 17.3 mph/1000 rpm in direct top gear, 21.6 mph/1000 rpm in overdrive top.
Suspension and brakes 9.7 in. diameter front disc brakes, 8 × 1.25 in. rear drum brakes. 5.60-13 in. tyres on 4.5 in. rim bolt-on steel disc wheels.
Dimensions Length 12 ft 9 in.; width 5 ft 0 in.; height 4 ft 4.5 in. Front track 4 ft 1 in.; rear track 4 ft 0 in. Unladen weight 2100 lb.

Convertible specification As for saloon, except for convertible body style.

Vitesse 2-litre Mk II

Vitesse 2-litre Mk II
Built July 1968 to May 1971
Number built 9121—5649 saloons, 3472 convertibles
Chassis numbers HC50001 to HC58109 inclusive
Basic and total price on introduction:

Saloon	£743	(Total £951)
Convertible	£780	(Total £999)

Saloon specification
Engine 6-cyl., in-line, cast-iron cylinder block and cylinder head, with four crankshaft main bearings. Bore, stroke and capacity 74.7 × 76.0 mm, 1998 cc (2.94 × 2.99 in., 122 cu in.). CR 9.25:1. Two horizontal constant-vacuum Zenith-Stromberg carburettors. 104 bhp (net) at 5300 rpm. Maximum torque 117 lb ft at 3000 rpm.
Transmission Final drive ratio 3.89:1. Overall gear ratios 3.89, 4.86, 6.92, 10.30, reverse 12.06:1. Synchromesh on all forward gears. Optional Laycock overdrive on top and third gears, overall ratios 3.11, and 3.93:1. 17.3 mph/1000 rpm in direct top gear, 21.6 mph/1000 rpm in overdrive top.
Suspension and brakes 9.7 in. diameter front disc brakes, 8 × 1.25 in. rear drum brakes. 155-13 in. radial ply tyres, on 4.5 in. rim bolt-on steel disc wheels. (Independent rear suspension by transverse leaf springs, lower wishbones, radius arm, and lever-arms hydraulic dampers on this model, alone of the entire family.)
Dimensions Length 12 ft 9 in.; width 5 ft 0 in.; height 4 ft 4.5 in. Front track 4 ft 1 in.; rear track 4 ft 0.5 in. Unladen weight 2044 lb.

Convertible specification As for saloon, except for convertible body style.

Chapter 9

13/60: the final years

By the end of 1963, Standard-Triumph was profitable again, and the figures were improving all the time. Leyland's investment was beginning to pay off, and Donald Stokes' confident smile was to be seen, more and more, in the press.

By this time, it was good news all the way for Triumph products. Every single new, or updated, model was selling well. The Spitfire had been an immediate success, the Americans seemed to like the TR4, and the Triumph 2000 saloon was just going on sale. The Vitesse, 12/50 and Herald models were all flooding out of the Canley factory; well over 2000 cars were being assembled in a good week.

Even so, and in spite of the fact that more than 57,000 Heralds and Vitesses had been produced in the 1962–63 financial year, the sales force were beginning to agitate for further improvements to the 1200 models. It was a period when minds were made up, then changed, very frequently. In the spring of 1963, for instance, it had been agreed that the new front-wheel-drive 'Ajax' model (which became Triumph 1300), would be launched in the autumn of 1965, that it *might* be produced in two-door and four-door saloon form, that it would be cheaper than the existing Herald, and that it would replace the Herald in any case.

By the spring of 1964, however, that strategy had been abandoned. The Herald was doing so well that it was decided to keep it on, and to run 'Ajax' as an altogether more costly, up-market, little car. In the autumn of 1964, therefore, Donald Stokes made an important announcement, ahead of the Earls Court Motor Show. Not only did he reveal an £8 million development programme and a plan to increase production by 15 per cent, but he also announced that production of the Herald range would continue for another five years:

'When the Herald was announced in 1959 it was greeted as a revolutionary car—it was the first British car in volume production to have all-independent suspension, featured unrivalled manoeuvrability, cheap and easy maintenance, a high safety characteristic and forward-looking styling.

'We believe that this formula is as valid today as it was then, and our sales support this belief.

'After a five-year production cycle it might be reasonable to expect a downward trend in sales, but the reverse is true of the Herald. It has proved itself as a top value-for-money vehicle, and demand is now running at a record level.'

The Herald, however, could not be expected to sell indefinitely without being improved, progressively, from time to time. The biggest deterrent to sales, the sales force insisted, was that the original front end was looking too craggy. Even in mid-1963 they had been asking for the Vitesse front end, or a modified version of it, to be fitted to export models, but this was turned down, in favour of the use of the more delicate 12/50 grille in the existing sheet metal.

Not even after Stanley Markland resigned at the end of 1963, to go into retirement, at which point Donald Stokes became the company's chairman, did the policy change. However, the fruits of Spitfire race and rally development became immediately apparent during 1964, for Harry Webster urged, and got, approval for a productionized eight-port cylinder head to be added to the engine. In 1.3-litre form, as proposed for the 'Ajax'/Triumph 1300 model, this would produce up to 65 bhp, he forecast.

Even before then, however, thoughts of facelifting the Herald had begun to surface. At a board meeting in May of that year, Donald Stokes said that 'we are considering a new face for the Herald', and that it was hoped to revamp the car in 12 months' time.

In fact, there was so much new model activity in the pipeline—the new 1300, the TR4A, and the GT6 among them—that this decision had to be put off. However, as it was clear that the engine would remain in production for a number of years, and because the machine tools were being regularly and seriously overworked, it was decided to spend £340,000 on refurbishing them.

By the beginning of 1966, however, there was no doubt that the Herald needed a facelift. 1200 and 12/50 sales had both been affected by the impact of the new front-wheel-drive 1300 (which my then colleagues on *Autocar* described as standing alone 'as the best small car currently available.') The company's planners, therefore, thought the existing car could hold up throughout 1966, but that a decline would then set in.

The directors, therefore, took several decisions—one was to push ahead with the idea of a Herald replacement (which would eventually appear as the rear-drive Toledo of mid-1970), the other was to give the existing car a thorough face-lift, and freshening up. It was not for nothing that Giovanni Michelotti's contract was revised, and made more lucrative for him, for the work-load put on him by Standard-Triumph, not to mention Leyland themselves, was now intense!

In the engine bay, the Herald 13/60 can immediately be identified by the use of the single, horizontal, Zenith-Stromberg carburettor and the pancake aircleaner outboard of it. The whole unit was nearly identical to that used in the front-drive Triumph 1300. Front wheel disc brakes, of course, had been standardised

A great deal of mind-changing then followed. At first the sales staff asked for the 1200 to be dropped in 1967, and for all cars to be upgraded to 12/50 specification (but without the sun-roof as standard), then they withdrew this request. Next, consideration was given to a longer wheelbase Herald, with an extra four inches added; although the first bodyshell was to have been ready by the spring of 1967, it was not completed. The tooling costs for a revised bodyshell would have been £1 million, and the project was scrapped. No photographs of this car seem to have survived.

Accordingly, in 1967 there was a concerted rush to get a facelifted car out for the Motor Show of that year, and this is how the 13/60 came into existence. It was all done in such a hurry that the experimental department only ever built three cars—one saloon, one convertible and one estate—all as converted 1200s, fresh from the assembly lines.

To keep the marketing strategy tidy, it was decided to drop the 12/50 model to make way for the new car, and to drop all but the 1200 saloon. For 1968, therefore, there was to be a 1200 saloon, along with 13/60 saloons, convertibles and estate cars.

Visually, the important change was to the nose, where the bare bones of the Vitesse bonnet were used, but with a new front panel, including large seven-inch headlamps, and a new stripey grille style. The only other external change was to include new boot lid badges. The number 13/60, incidentally, was really no more than engineering short-hand for the new power unit, a 1300 cc, 60 bhp, unit.

The Herald 1200, of course, had been launched with 39 bhp, while the 12/50 had 51 bhp. Later, actually from November 1964, in an unannounced change, the 12/50's camshaft (but not the higher compression ratio head) was applied to the 1200, whose power then rose

A busy Triumph factory scene in Coventry, showing that there was no bodyshell segregation into model families before trimming and assembly began. In shot here are 13/60s, Spitfires, GT6s, and Triumph 2000s. The date is late 1967

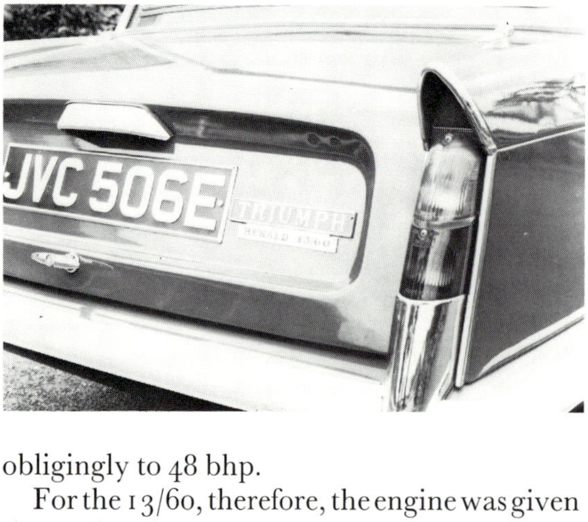

ABOVE *To increase the space in the back seat of the 13/60, not only were the seats pushed back, and down, but elbow spaces were scooped out of the trim panels to each side. Compare this with . . .*

CENTRE LEFT . . . *the treatment of the same corner in the Vitesse 2-litre, announced a year earlier*

TOP LEFT *The 13/60's instrument display was very smart, and used components from the front-drive 1300 model. It was a very neat, pleasing, and ergonomic layout*

TOP RIGHT *For the 13/60, a particularly neat facelift of the Herald front end was devised, using Vitesse pressings, but only single seven inch headlamps, instead of the twin lamps used in the Vitesse itself*

LEFT *13/60 badging, of a type stylistically the same as that of the 1300 models*

obligingly to 48 bhp.

For the 13/60, therefore, the engine was given the 1296 cc size already applied to the Spitfire 3, and to the 1300 saloon. In conjunction with this, there was the new eight-port cylinder head, an 8.5:1 compression ratio, the same camshaft profile as before and a single horizontal Zenith-Stromberg 150CD carburettor, and AC paper-element air cleaner, on the more efficient-looking manifolds also to be found in the 1300 saloon. The result was a peak output of 61 bhp (net) at 5000 rpm (27 per cent better than that of the 1200, 20 per cent better than that of the 12/50), and a meaty 73 lb ft of torque at 3000 rpm.

Behind the engine, the diaphragm spring clutch, and the gearbox were as before, but the rear suspension output shafts were beefed up, to accord with those of the latest Spitfire and Vitesse cars. Apart from the use of the Spitfire 3's front disc calipers as standard (which were larger than those previously fitted to the 12/50), there were no chassis changes, for narrow 3.5 in. rim wheels were retained on the saloons and Convertibles (4.5 in. rims on the Estate car), along with cross-ply tyres.

Compared with the 12/50, the interior was freshened up, notably on the facia, where Triumph 1300-style instruments and switch-gear had been adopted. Front seats were recontoured, but more work had gone into the rear compartment, where the apex of the squab and cushion had been moved downwards and backwards to give an extra two inches of legroom, and there was extra elbow room provided by the adoption of scooped out recesses in the panels to each side of the back seat, but only in the saloons because the engineering of the convertible hoods and estate car floors precluded the improvement on the other models.

The prices for 1968 (with 12/50 prices in brackets) were as follows:

1200 saloon	£627
13/60 saloon	£700 (£678)
13/60 Convertible	£755
13/60 Estate	£774

The factory made much of the fact that the 13/60, though highly-specified, and a much better car than the original 948 cc car in every way, still cost only £75 more, in basic terms, after eight years. (Indeed, because of the reductions in purchase tax made, the 13/60 was actually £2 cheaper than the original car, in overall terms!)

Sir Donald Stokes (he had been knighted in 1965) was predictably bullish about the new model in his welcome to the press, reminding them all that nearly half a million Heralds had already been built, that it was the most successful car Standard-Triumph had ever produced, and that it was currently being assembled, not only in the UK, but in countries as varied as Belgium, Australia, Portugal, New Zealand, Peru and India. The Standard Triumph Review of November 1967 headlined their description with the phrase: More Power to your Elbow.

Would the customers like the new cars? They did. Right away, the production rate of saloons perked up from the 600/month of the 12/50s to 1200/1300 a month for the 13/60s, while the well-liked Herald 1200 saloon continued at around 800 a month. The rejuvenation had worked well.

The 13/60, in any case, was a much quicker car than before. In recording its opinions of March 1968, *Autocar* magazine made it clear that the car was almost as quick as the original Spitfire had been in 1962, and that was a sports car! After all, with a top speed of 84 mph, 0–60 mph acceleration in 17.7 seconds, and an overall fuel consumption of 28.3 mpg, it was quite a package.

The testers summarized that: 'There is still no car with a more accessible engine and front assembly . . . Michelotti has transformed the frontal appearance of the 13/60, making it distinctive and pleasing in 1968. There is no other model completely competitive with this Herald, and at its price it is still a good buy.'

This summarized what many motorists must have thought, in spite of the enormous choice of models they now had in any Standard-Triumph showroom.

It was that choice, more than the competition from outside, which did so much to give the 13/60 a hard time, for the 1300 saloon had also been joined by the 1300TC, with more power and performance than before. It is worth noting, by the way, the line-up of saloons available from Triumph after the 1968 Motor Show, when the Mk 2 Vitesse 2-litre had been launched. These, and their prices, were as follows:

Herald 1200	£684
Herald 13/60	£761
1300	£917
1300TC	£959
Vitesse 2-litre Mk 2	£970
2000	£1297

TOP LEFT *There was a full range of 13/60s from 1967 to 1971. This was the saloon . . .*

TOP RIGHT . . . *which contrasts well with the convertible, still popular after all those years . . .*

ABOVE . . . *and the practical estate car derivative*

By 1970, however, the entire Herald/Vitesse family was in steady, and quite unstoppable, decline. Way back in the mid-1960s, the decision had been made to concentrate on developments of the 1300 family of cars. By 1970, the company was ready to launch the rear-drive Toledo as something of a Herald replacement, with the front-drive 1500 taking over from the 1300/1300TC models, and coming along was the 1.85-litre overhead-cam engined Dolomite, to replace the Vitesse.

Accordingly, sales of the 1200 and the 13/60 gradually fell away. Only 9292 1200s were built in 1968, 5625 in 1969, and a mere 1845 in 1970. The last of all was built in May 1970, by which time production of Toledos had already begun.

The 13/60 fared better, as well it might, and the figures show that no fewer than 28,610 cars were built in 1968, followed by 21,692 in 1969, and 20,311 in 1970. However, once the Toledo had appeared, even the 13/60 was under sentence of death. Although a large number of saloons (1707) were completed in October 1970, and a further 1217 in November, quite suddenly it was all over in December, and only the convertibles and estate cars carried on into 1971. As with the 2-litre Vitesse of the day, though, these cars were living on borrowed time, and the final examples were assembled at the same time, in May 1971.

Although this was the end of the separate-chassis Heralds and Vitesses at Canley, it was not the end for the basic layout. The Herald—or more strictly, the Standard Gazel—continued to be built in India for some time, while in the UK the GT6 sports Coupé was built until the end of 1973, and the extremely popular Spitfire was in full production until the end of 1980.

All in all, I am sure, the Herald family was extremely profitable to Standard-Triumph, but it is easy to see why the separate-chassis experiment was never taken up by any other European manufacturer. The good news for preservation enthusiasts, of course, was that the separate-chassis design proved to be more long-lasting than a conventional monocoque, and the result was that a high proportion of the cars survived into the mid and late 1970s, without rust corrosion killing them off.

Facts and figures: Herald 13/60

Facts and figures: Herald 13/60
Built August 1967 to May 1971
Number built 67,672—40,433 saloons, 11,772 Convertibles, and 15,467 Estates
Chassis numbers GE1 to GE83433 inclusive
Basic and total price on introduction:

saloon	£568	(Total £700)**
Convertible	£613	(Total £755)
Estate	£628	(Total £774)

**Note that purchase tax rates had once again changed. The total price was 123 per cent of basic, compared with 121 per cent for the original 12/50, and 142 per cent for the original 1200!

Saloon specification
Engine 4-cyl., in-line, cast-iron cylinder block and cylinder head, with three crankshaft main bearings. Bore, stroke and capacity 73.7 × 76 mm, 1296 cc (2.90 × 2.99 in., 79.1 cu in.). CR 8.5:1, one Zenith-Stromberg horizontal constant-vacuum carburettor. 61 bhp (net) at 5000 rpm. Maximum torque 73 lb ft at 3000 rpm.
Transmission Final drive ratio 4.11:1. Overall gear ratios 4.11, 5.74, 8.88, 15.42, reverse 15.42:1. Synchromesh on top, third and second gears. 15.7 mph/1000 rpm in top gear.
Suspension and brakes 9 in. front disc brakes, 7 × 1.25 in. rear drum brakes. 5.20-13 in. tyres on 3.5 in. rim bolt-on steel disc wheels.
Dimensions Length 12 ft 9 in.; width 5 ft 0 in.; height 4 ft 4 in. Front track 4 ft 1 in.; rear track 4 ft 0 in. Unladen weight 1876 lb.

Convertible specification As for saloon, except for convertible body style. Unladen weight 1820 lb.

Estate specification As for saloon, except for estate body style, 5.60-13 in. tyres on 4.5 in. rim wheels. Unladen weight 1988 lb.

No coupé derivative of the 13/60 was ever officially produced.

Chapter 10
Herald and Vitesse in the USA

When Standard-Triumph launched the Herald at Palm Springs, California in early 1960, it seemed as if they'd captured two new markets: econocars and sporty compacts. The Herald saloon, though $200–300 more expensive than a Renault Dauphine or VW Beetle, had more room, performance and luxury than those two formidable rivals. Against the popular sporty derivatives, the VW Karmann Ghia and Renault Caravelle, Triumph had the Herald Coupé and Convertible, priced $200–400 *below* them. Since Americans were buying VWs and Renaults at the rate of more than 200,000 a year, of which a healthy 15,000 were Ghias and Caravelles, the Herald range seemed likely to steal some sales in two burgeoning fields.

Triumph had tried to crack the US small car market before, with the lamentable Mayflower and the badge-engineered Standard Ten (Triumph Ten in USA). Neither had sold well, the Mayflower because it cost almost as much as a Chevrolet, the Ten because it was ugly, buzzy and more costly than a Beetle.

Compared to those predecessors the Herald seemed almost space-age. It had four-wheel independent suspension, a remarkably small turning circle, hardly any grease fittings, novel extruded aluminium bumpers, and a bonnet/wing unit that swung up to provide unlimited engine accessibility. But, with a conventional front-mounted, watercooled engine driving the rear wheels, it was clearly familiar to Americans.

The sporty Herald models also had something Renault and VW lacked: the magic name of a sports car, proven through countless successes on road, track and rally course. The Karmann Ghia and Caravelle (Floride in Europe) had never been able to pass themselves off as sports cars (not through want of trying). One would be hard pressed to call any Herald a sports car either, but at least it was related to one.

Unfortunately, the Herald came along about two years too late, just as America's Big Three had girded themselves to build what they euphemistically called 'compacts'. The Valiant, Corvair and Falcon weren't by any means as small as the Herald, but they didn't cost a lot more, and were sold by more dealers, most of whom were familiar to their customers. The import market fell apart in 1961 as the supply of American 'compacts' increased, and some imports never recovered. In 1960 Renault had sold one car for every three Volkswagens; by 1966 there was only one for every 12, and Triumph was outselling Renault. The French have never enjoyed a larger piece of the American pie since, which is probably why they decided to buy a US company in the 1970s.

For most imports the early 1960s were spent climbing back from the initial surge of domestic small cars. (Detroit helped by gradually making the 'compacts' bigger.) Triumph in particular benefited during this recovery, thanks to the new TR4 and Spitfire as well as the Herald line. By 1964 Standard-Triumph was outselling Renault and ranked second to VW in important car sales in America. S-T remained number two through 1966, something that seems hard to imagine in this day of Japanese dominance. Of course, it only took

The 948 cc Herald in typical USA guise with wide whitewalls. (This was the last year for 'wide whites'; Detroit switched to narrow-bands in 1963 and the imports followed suit.) Another detail change, the forerunner of massive regulation to come, was the advent of amber front trafficators in 1963. This car was the last year Herald with the all-white lenses

The slow-selling Herald coupé as presented in America, most often with whitewall tyres. Standard-Triumph unloaded only 1049 of these in three years, although they sold for less and performed better than the popular VW Karmann Ghia

21,314 sales to achieve this position in 1964, and meanwhile VW was selling over 300,000.

But the Triumph Herald proved a lot less successful than its builders had hoped. In the early 1960s it was arguably the worst time to be bringing in economy imports, and the cars shipped over from Coventry were not the best of Triumphs. 'They were very poorly built,' says a former Triumph executive—'real junk, to be honest. The situation wasn't helped by all the work we had to do to make them saleable when they got here. Because the market was bad, many cars were just stored under England's sunny skies—that meant they had to be repainted in whole or in part before we could put them on a US salesfloor.'

From a product planning standpoint, too, the line-up was weak. When the Herald Estate came along in 1961, S-T/USA made the decision not to import it, yet there's no doubt that it would have sold better than the Coupé. Triumph's emphasis on sporty bodies no doubt stemmed from a desire to capitalize on the TR reputation, but compared to the Ghia and Caravelle, the Herald Coupé and Convertible just looked peculiar. Although Triumph eventually sold close to 16,000 of its sporty body styles, the Karmann Ghia was accounting for as many as 38,825 US sales per year, and was the second most popular two-seater in America next to the Chevrolet Corvette. The Herald Convertible sold fairly well, but for VW, Ghia coupés outsold ragtops five to one, and this percentage of closed to open car sales was hardly atypical. Leaving all other factors aside, the Karmann Ghia coupé was pretty, while the Herald Coupé was at best odd looking, at worst ugly. The fact that it sold for about $400 less than the Ghia coupé was incidental, because if an American could spend $2200 on a car in the 1960s, he could probably spend $2600 without much strain.

In performance and handling, there wasn't much to choose from between the Herald and its major European rivals. All three rode full independent suspensions, all three were sluggish performers by American standards, and all three oversteered with abandon. The Herald's unpredictability in the wet was a definite disadvantage in a country where the nuances of automobile handling are not generally appreciated. The Herald rode a little better than the VW or Renault, but not enough to impress people. It had more interior and boot space than its rivals, and the evidence is that this *did* help sales, but interior space doesn't rank very high among the criteria that govern buyers' decisions, at least in the economy sector.

And in the long run, the Herald would suffer from the same problems that plagued Renault and many other imports in America: the lack of dealer backing, parts and service. In the United States in the late 1950s and 1960s, VW service was legendary. The factory took huge pains qualifying dealers; it insisted that they sell nothing but VWs, that they carry a minimum supply of parts, that they train and keep training all their mechanics. Too often your friendly neighbourhood Triumph dealer was a fellow who sold mostly Oldsmobiles, for whom Triumph was very much secondary—with all that implies about parts and service. The 948 cc Heralds were poorly assembled and proved highly susceptible to rust. This was anathema in America, where winters are severe in some places and road salt is an everyday fact of life from November to March. VWs rusted too, and Ghias could dissolve before one's eyes, but Americans were so hooked on VW that they traded old ones in on new ones regularly, so many never realized the problem. It was easier, too, to replace a rotted VW wing, since it required a mere bolt-on installation; badly rusted Heralds were more complicated.

It is to Triumph's credit that management quickly saw the deficiencies of product in the 948 cc line, and moved fast to do something about it. What S-T called the 'Herald 1200' and later just the 1200, began arriving in March 1961. There was in fact some sales overlap between this new-generation Herald and the original—but there was no comparison.

The 948 cc car was less than ideal for American conditions, notably because of its relatively low maximum cruising speed. Whereas a VW could cruise easily at its top speed, just 60 mph in a 948 cc Herald required 4400 rpm, thanks to its low 4.875:1 axle ratio. At 70 mph, which at that time was the legal speed on many American highways, the Herald turned 5150 rpm. 'It is all very well to prattle on about engines that will "run all day" at 5000 rpm,' said *Road & Track*, 'but the average car owner is much more interested in driving all year at 3500 rpm. For that reason, the original Herald had a somewhat limited usefulness and the happiest of its owners were those who bought it for urban-type driving, where the cruising speeds are moderate.'

The new Herald 1200 was a major improvement for American buyers. Not only was its displacement increased by about 20 per cent; its axle ratio was now 4.11:1, a 16 per cent drop. This did nothing for acceleration—in fact the 1200 was a bit slower off the mark—but it raised the cruising speed considerably, and 70 mph now required only 4460 rpm. Like changes were made in the 1200's gear ratios.

American testers found these all to the good. 'In the earlier Herald, the transmission ratios were staged so that 1st and 2nd gears were close, with a long gap to 3rd and 4th,' wrote *Road & Track*. 'The revised ratios give a nice, even progression through the gears and are, in fact, better staged than many of those in out-and-out sports cars. Stirring the gears about was a pleasure, due to the precise action of the shift lever and the effectiveness of the synchromesh.'

The 1200 was improved in other ways that appealed to US buyers. The old seats, which were virtual benches, narrow and rather hard, were reshaped to provide more lateral support, and given more padding plus a rake adjustment. The steering column, adjustable on the 1200, was better able to handle gangling Yanks or their 4 ft 10 in. lady friends as the case may be. The walnut veneer dash looked far better than the old Herald's moulded-fibre, and the white-on-black instruments were more purposeful than the hard-to-read white-faced gauges of the past. One carried-over feature that was always an important one for Herald salesmen was the limited lubrication requirement: two chassis fittings needed attention at 6000 miles, four more at 12,000 miles. At a time when the typical car still bristled with 1000-mile-interval grease fittings, this was an important sales factor. Not to be overlooked,

ABOVE *New England setting for the Herald 1200, later known simply as the 1200 in the USA (possibly because 'Herald' did not denote much of a reputation – the early 948 cc cars were poorly put together). Full wheel covers and whitewalls were usually added to suit then-current buyer preference*

RIGHT *Press preview of the Sports Six for east coast writers at the Tavern on the Green, Central Park, New York City, autumn 1962. Much more elegant looking, the Vitesse fascinated road testers in America, but its $2500 price put off most customers*

Standard-Triumph had also cut the price of the base Herald saloon to just under $1700—a lot closer to VW and therefore a lot more competitive. The Coupé, which hadn't sold at all well, was dropped in the US, but the Convertible was also cut in price, to just under $2000. The price cuts and the product improvements were what helped bring Standard-Triumph sales to a decade high 21,214 in the United States during calendar year 1964, and enabled S-T to surpass Renault as the number-two importer.

With the Spitfire and TR4 firmly established by 1963, the company decided to expand its US sales effort by importing the convertible model of the Triumph Vitesse, called 'Sports 6' in the United States. This was a shrewd decision, because the Sports 6 eliminated most of the Herald's outstanding sales problems in America. Its lovely 1.6-litre six-cylinder engine was more than capable of cruising US interstate highways in company with the Cadillacs and Lincolns and Imperials, and its 0–60 time of about 17 seconds was adequate if not spectacular. Moreover, the Sports 6 *looked* much better, Triumph having replaced the peculiar 'buttercup' headlamps of the Herald with a set of canted quad lights, built into a smoother looking front end. Wisely, too, they held the price down: the Sports 6 convertible listed at $2500, which was hardly more than the $2229 asked for the original Herald Convertible, factored for inflation, and well under the price of a Karmann Ghia soft-top.

By just about every American road tester's measurement the Sports 6 was unique.

'Standard-Triumph has made an outstanding car which does not belong in any normal category,' remarked *Car and Driver*. '[The] exceptionally smooth and economical engine gives it a top speed of 97 mph. The company has not broken new ground in creating the Sports 6, for the small six-cylinder models were popular in England during the 1930s, but must be complimented for re-introducing it.'

One could question whether a small six was as necessary in the 1960s as it was in the 1930s. We had learned a great deal about engine mounting methods and materials in the 30 intervening years, which had done much to hide the inherent secondary harmonic unbalance of four-cylinder engines. But as *C and D* concluded, 'the six-cylinder unit nevertheless offers better balance and improved smoothness, detectable even by passengers, which helps reduce noise and vibration throughout the drive train.' And that was important in America, where people were used to being cushioned inside a silent, rolling womb, surrounded by acres of sheet metal. (We have since become a lot less encapsulated, thankfully.)

Standard-Triumph did not, however, expect to sell many Sports 6s, and so geared its promotion. 'It is a limited-edition car for those who seek true sports car performance, maximum safety and room for the whole family,' said S-T Inc. president Martin J. Tustin. One suspects they missed the boat, although judgement is always much better in hindsight. But in the end Standard-Triumph sold only 679 Sports 6 Convertibles, according to their longtime PR manager Mike Cook, and the model remained peripheral at most S-T showrooms.

S-T's reasoning had to do with the state of domestic competition. By 1963 every Detroit manufacturer had a veritable fleet of small cars—not as small as the Herald/Sports 6, but considered 'compact' by Americans. And if $2500 sounds cheap by today's standards, one must remember that a Dodge Dart convertible cost only $2389 at the same time. After Ford introduced the Mustang in Spring 1964, any thoughts about increasing Sports 6 volume in the USA must have disappeared, since you could buy a Mustang convertible for only $2722—and that *included* the V8 engine. The Sports 6 was too pricey.

None of which takes credit away from Standard-Triumph for having the intelligence to combine the Vanguard six with the Herald body in the first place. The result was a pleasant car, with plenty of power, surprising smoothness, agility and a deal of luxury. (One could even order air conditioning on US models.) But the package might have been more successful, and put a larger dent in the US import market, had the Sports 6 come along before the Herald in America.

By late 1964 Standard-Triumph Inc. stopped importing the Sports 6 and restricted its small car effort to the 1200 saloon and Convertible—mainly the latter. Over its eight years on the US market the 1200 Convertible accounted for almost three of every four 1200 sales. To try to pump up the saloon end, Triumph began importing the larger 2000 in 1966. The 2000 made more sense than the Sports 6 and stood to sell many more copies, since it was a four-door sedan. At $2895 it was priced to compete with the luxury compacts. That the 2000 didn't succeed is a greater tragedy than the failure of the Sports 6, but this is another story.

Standard-Triumph retained the 1200 through 1967, cutting the price still further to $1665 for the saloon and $1909 for the convertible. The soft-top was now the cheapest open model on the American market, and a spectacular buy: toward the end of 1967 it was outselling the saloon by five or six to one. But overall, annual 1200 sales were negligible, and the sports cars carried the overhead. Total Triumph sales in the USA dropped by one-third between 1964 and 1967, and in this last year Renault once again outsold Triumph, on the strength of its new R8.

Nineteen sixty-seven was a watershed year for imports in the United States because it was the last year before government safety and emissions regulations. These rapidly became stiffer in the 1970s. The advent of regulation caused many a European manufacturer to rethink its approach to the US market and some—like Morgan—to give up altogether. Triumph was thinking with the rest of them, and the upshot was a firm decision to sink or swim exclusively with sports cars. Accordingly, the 1968 Triumph range was bereft of sedans: both the 2000 and the Herald 1200 got the axe, and Standard-Triumph offered the sports car threesome of TR250, Spitfire and GT6. Retaining the Spitfire meant that they had a suitably detoxed four-cylinder engine for the 1200, but to keep it would have involved more than engine mods. 'Safety' was now a very big fetish, and before long that would include special bumpers, expensive crash and pendulum tests, and a plethora of buttons, bells, warning lights, buzzers, and things that go bump in the night. Standard-Triumph USA decided that the volume of Herald 1200 sales in America just didn't warrant the effort, and Standard-Triumph were right.

The whole Herald idea was really becoming outmoded by the late 1960s, and not just in America. Even when it was fresh, the Herald was bucking a worldwide trend toward concentrating engines and drive wheels in one spot, either the front or the back. To this extent, and its many novel features aside, it represented technology of the past. How could it otherwise, since it was designed in the 1950s? Even so it was a good and interesting product that became continually better as the years passed, and its Vitesse/Sports 6 evolution was an exciting development in the small four-seater field. In America it deserved better than it got: lacklustre service and lukewarm promotion. It played second fiddle not only to the Triumph sports cars, but to the big Detroit balloons with which it shared floor space. Still, it made a lot of American friends, and some of them are still around, driving Heralds to Triumph club rallies and showing off the occasional pristine Sports 6. It could have been worse.

The Sports 6 as Standard-Triumph wished to visualise it, carefree second car transport for affluent American suburbia. This car still bears the wide whitewall tyres, which gradually were replaced by 'narrow bands' in 1963. Unfortunately, US suburbia bought Chevy Nova, Corvair, Falcon, Valiant and Dart convertibles instead, usually for less than the price of the Sports 6

Facts and figures: Herald, 1200, Sports 6 in America: prices and sales

	*Price**	*Sales*
Herald (948 cc): *March 60–March 62*		
saloon	$1849	3612
Coupé	$2149	1049
Convertible	$2229	2822
Herald 1200: *March 61–March 68*		
saloon	$1699/1665	4609
Convertible	$1949/1909	11,654
Sports 6: *Sept. 62–Sept. 64*		
Convertible	$2499	679

Comparisons 1960	*Herald*	*VW Karmann Ghia*	*Renault Caravelle*
Coupé price*	$2149	$2535	$2445
Convertible price*	$2229	$2795	$2395
wheelbase (in.)	91.5	94.5	89.0
bhp (net)	45	38	40
0–60 mph (sec., ave)	25	28	27
mpg US gal.)	30	31	37

Comparisons 1963	*Herald*	*Chevrolet Corvair*	*Ford Falcon*
Convertible price*	$1949	$2481	$2470
wheelbase (in.)	91.5	108.0	109.5
bhp (net)	39	71	76
0–60 mph (secs., ave)	23.0	16.5	16.0
mpg (US gal.)	30	22	25
Top speed	80	87	88

*Prices POE East Coast

Triumph trumpeted its neat air conditioning installation, shown here on a Herald, which was designed and manufactured in Pennsylvania. By the mid-Sixties the cost of 'refrigeration' had become low enough for most buyers to afford it, and air conditioning installations soared; even VW was offering the accessory by 1965.

Footnote

This chapter was prepared by acknowledged Triumph expert in North America, Richard Langworth.

Chapter 11

Close relatives: Bond Equipe, and the specials

Not long after the Herald was put on to the market, the various special builders began to use its components. Up to the end of the 1950s, Ford and BMC had provided most of the 'building blocks'—engine, transmissions, steering and suspension units—but now there was a modern, and very attractive alternative.

Many builders, for sure, wanted to use the entire Herald chassis and running gear, but Standard-Triumph were not willing to make them available. On the other hand, they were quite ready to supply the 'bit and pieces'. In the next few years, Herald rack-and-pinion steering, Herald front suspension components, and the chassis-mounted differential, all became familiar to non-Triumph owners.

Alford and Alder, who manufactured all of the Herald's front suspension, drummed up a lot of business over the years, most glamorously in connection with the 1960s Lotus road cars—Elan, Plus 2, and Europa—and for literally hundreds of single-seater racing cars. The Herald's suspension vertical link was an ideal size, and layout, for many race car suspensions (though these cars often had specially-designed wishbones). It featured on early-1960s Formula 1 cars, even, but was to be found on Formula 2, 3, Junior and Ford single-seaters right through the decade.

For some years, however, Standard-Triumph refused to make the complete chassis available to any outside concern, if only because it would be competition for their own products. Anyone dropping a specially-styled sports body on to a Herald chassis might have harmed the Spitfire's prospects, if only to a limited degree, and there would certainly have been an effect on the sales of Herald Coupés and Convertibles.

Until, that is, the factory received a serious approach from Bond Cars, of Preston, in Lancashire. There were dealer connections, through common directors, with a Standard-Triumph distributor in Lancashire, which must have helped, but Bond's proposal was eventually taken seriously when it was seen that their proposed new car was not likely to be in competition with the Herald, but could be sold as a complementary model to it.

Bond had been building motorcycle engined three-wheelers since 1948, but it was not until the beginning of the 1960s that managing director Tom Gratrix saw the three-wheeler market (protected by favourable annual tax levels) drifting steadily downhill. A new Bond car project—actually the first four-wheeler to be designed by this modest little concern—then began to evolve at the beginning of 1962. The thought was that such a car would have to be a 'gap-filler' in any car manufacturer's range, and would have to be built with their co-operation.

First thoughts were for a car to use Ford Anglia 105E/Classic 109E parts; this, and a later scheme to use BMC A-Series engines, both collapsed on commercial grounds. It was not until Gratrix put the idea to Standard-Triumph that everything began to look encouraging. For Bond, in fact, Leyland's ownership of Standard-Triumph was to their advantage, because they had been close geographical neighbours for some years, while Bond's parent company, Loxhams (also Stan-

Using the Herald chassis and running gear, with Spitfire-tune engine, was the Bond Equipe GT, which also used the Herald's scuttle/firewall, and modified doors. The rest of the bodywork was in fibreglass

dard-Triumph distributors) were well-respected by the hard-headed truck-building colossus.

Tom Gratrix was quoted, at the time, that: 'We knew there were enough keen motorists around, from frustrated family men with sports car inclinations to spirited lasses who wanted to drive in a lovely manner without having their hairdos blown about, who would gladly pay a little bit extra. . . .'

As *Motor* later said, in a review of the Bond project: 'What made the prospect more interesting was that no manufacturer, Standard-Triumph included, had considered there was sufficient production potential for their assembly lines in a small, grand tourer of outstanding styling which would combine the comfort and most of the roominess of a saloon, with the handling and performance characteristics . . . of the two-seater sports car.'

The first Herald-chassis'd Bond, the Equipe GT, was announced in May 1963, and I see that in a later Bond feature in *Autocar* I described it as 'a clever cocktail of Herald, Spitfire and Vitesse parts, to be called the Equipe GT 2 + 2. With the Herald Coupé out of production, the Equipe fulfilled a real need.'

At first the new car was described as being built in association with Standard-Triumph, for it was not until late in 1963 that the Bond concern was given an exclusive three-year licencing agreement to use so much of the Herald/Vitesse/Spitfire in its product.

None of the Bonds built in the next seven years used standard rolling chassis, for each model had different components tailored to the whole. The original Equipe, for instance, used a Herald chassis, but a Spitfire engine (of 63 bhp) of 1147 cc, disc front brakes as standard, and Vitesse instrument panel and wheel trims. The components, in fact, were shipped up the new M6 motorway from Coventry to Preston for assembly in Preston, after which the completed cars were sold through selected Standard-

The Equipe GT4S came along in 1964, complete with a four-headlamp nose, an opening boot lid, and more back seat headroom. The 1296 cc engine followed in 1965

Triumph distributors. Suspension settings were claimed to have been modified, to suit the new Bond, which was heavier than the Spitfire (at 1650 lb), but lighter than any of the Herald 1200s, while a wooden-rimmed steering wheel was standard.

The Equipe's body was fascinating, not only for its style, but for its construction. Although the front and rear of the shell were pure Bond, and were built from fibre glass, the scuttle, windscreen surround, floor and the doors themselves, together with windscreen and door mechanisms, were all Herald items. The rear quarters, the steeply sloping roof, and the lift up bonnet exterior were all produced by Bond, though even the inside of the bonnet was also modified from that of the Herald itself.

Inside the car, the facia was a modified Vitesse unit, with Spitfire instruments (including a rev-counter) built into it, by special arrangement with the normal facia suppliers to Standard-Triumph, while figure-hugging Microcell front seats were fitted. As with the original Standard Eight, and the original Austin-Healey Sprite, there was no external boot access; to load one's luggage, it was necessary to scramble in through the passenger doors, and fold down the rear seat's back rest.

The Equipe GT 2+2 had a neat and definitely sporty style, and performed very well, as independent road tests confirmed. At a time when the Herald 1200's normal top speed was just over 75 mph, and that of the Vitesse 1600 was still less than 90 mph, the Bond dropped neatly in between, with an 82 mph top speed, and 0–60 mph acceleration in about 17–18 seconds, which was roughly comparable with that of the Spitfire.

The Equipe, of course, was sold only as a completely built-up car (*never* as a kitcar), and was backed by the normal Standard-Triumph maker's warranty. It was priced at £822.23 (£680 without British purchase tax), at a time when the Herald 1200 cost £579 (£479), and the Vitesse 1600 cost £745 (£616). Clearly,

Not only did Bond produce a smart Equipe GT 2-litre model in the autumn of 1967, which had a fibreglass body sitting on the Vitesse 2-litre chassis, but a year later it became 'Mk II' with the 2-litre Mk 2 chassis and suspension, and at the same time a convertible model was made. Wire wheels were optional

One of the many 'specials' to use Herald running gear was this Moss sports car, seen at the Stoneleigh show of 1984. The basic style looks like that of an MG TF, and the radiator grille is from a 2½-litre Daimler V8-250 saloon

Bond could not hope to approach Triumph production levels, but geared themselves up to produce 20 cars a week. Even so, within two years, it was being advertised for sale in 26 countries by Standard-Triumph concessionaires.

In fact the original Equipe GT was short-lived. Customer response showed that a separate, exterior access, boot, was needed, along with more rear-seat space. Accordingly, from October 1964, the GT 2 + 2 was dropped, and a new derivative, titled the GT4S, took over. The 4S, naturally, meant 'four-seater'.

Mechanically, there were no changes for the time being (though the more powerful, 67 bhp, Spitfire Mk 2 engine would be standardized from the spring of 1965). The bodyshell was face-lifted, with a new four-headlamp nose (the lamp clusters were actually from the Triumph 2000), the rear of the roof line was raised to provide more headroom, and swept down less abruptly, across the new lockable boot lid, to a neat transverse spoiler. As before, the bodies were produced in a converted cotton mill, while final assembly was at Ribbleton Lane, Preston. On announcement, the 4S was priced at £817 (£675 without tax)—a £30 increase over the last of the Equipe GTs. Not only had there been an Equipe price reduction as sales volumes built up, but the 4S was brought in at a lower price than the original model!

The 4S, renamed 1300 when the enlarged 1296 cc Spitfire Mk 3 engine was fitted from the spring of 1967, then carried on, visually little changed, until 1970, always costing more than the equivalent Herald, and always selling in the same numbers. A study of chassis number sequences suggests that 544 of the original Bond Equipes, and no fewer than 2505 of the quad-headlamp 4S/1300 versions were built. Very good business, indeed, for Standard-Triumph, even if the production volume slowed down considerably after the end of 1967.

The reason for the slowing down was undoubtedly because of the second Triumph-based model to be produced by Bond—the Equipe 2-litre GT. Knowing the existing association between Sharps Commercials, who owned Bond, and Standard-Triumph, and seeing the title of the new car, it was not difficult to guess what was hidden away under the skin—it was, of course, a lightly-modified Vitesse 2-litre rolling chassis.

The mechanical specification, in fact, was almost pure Vitesse 2-litre, except for the trimming off of the chassis front cross-rail, and the rear side-member extensions (both to suit the differing requirements of Bond's own body), along with revision of spring and damper rates, and the offering of wire-spoke wheels as options (and radial ply tyres as standard). The 1998 cc engine produced 95 bhp, the gearbox was all-synchromesh, with optional overdrive, and the final-drive ratio was 3.89:1.

The body style, however, was completely new, entirely different from that of the Equipe GT 4S, and much more visually attractive. Bond started from the basis of a Triumph Vitesse body platform, scuttle, inner rear wheel-arches, and door inners (all, of course, being in pressed steel), and went their own way from there.

New Bond-designed steel pressings were used for the outer door panels, there were steel front inner wheelarches (ex-Triumph), and a steel rear bulkhead/parcel shelf. In addition, Bond provided longer, re-raked, windscreen pillars, so that a much larger windscreen glass could be fitted. Bonnet moulding, roof, tail and rear quarters were all in fibreglass, and there was a Herald Estate car petrol tank tucked away under the floor.

Like the GT4S, the 2-litre was a close coupled four-seater, with a Vitesse 2-litre facia/instrument panel, a GT6 steering wheel, and specially-shaped front seats developed from the GT6 components. The style featured crisp body lines, a four headlamp nose (the Triumph 2000, once again, being the component provider), adequate headroom over the rear seats, and a long sweep down to the tail, with a small opening boot lid between the backlight glass, and the rear bumper.

The price, on announcement in August 1967, was £1095.67 (£890, basic, without tax), which compared rather badly with the £839 (£681) asked of the Vitesse 2-litre, or the £985 (£800) asked of the GT6 of the day. Even so, Bond were nothing if not optimistic, even going so far as to advertise their new model thus:

'Is this the most beautiful car in the country?'

Like the Vitesse 2-litre, the Equipe 2-litre GT suffered criticism regarding its on-the-limit handling, so the Preston firm were doubtlessly happy to launch a Mark 2 version, complete with the new 'lower-wishbone' Vitesse 2-litre rear suspension, and with the uprated 104 bhp engine from that car; the styling, too, was set off by the dummy Rostyle wheel trims (known as 'Magnum' wheel trims) also to be found on the latest Vitesse.

The real headline-catcher at the 1968 Motor Show, however, was the new convertible version of the car, which was something of a surprise, as the convertible, in general, was accepted to be dying out. It was smart, and it was practical, but it was by no means cheap. As *Autocar* said in its road test, dated 8 May 1969:

'Don't look too close, though, as you may be disappointed at the standard of finish. And stand well clear when you mention the price, because everyone is going to whistle through their teeth at you and shake their head tut-tuttingly. . . .'

The convertible, in fact, was priced at £1313.73 (£998 without tax), at a time when you could have bought a new Vitesse 2-litre Mk 2 convertible for just £1019 (£780), and that put it into the MGC, TR6 and (almost) the Morgan Plus 8 bracket.

Argue about the price if you like (and there was no doubt that this put off many people), but you could not argue about the cars' performance. Top speed was about 102–105 mph, with acceleration to match. In other words, the Equipe 2-litre was just as fast as the Vitesse, but with a great deal of individual flair, and rust-free style.

Before the end, 590 Equipe 2-litre Mk 1s, and 841 Mk 2s were produced—so that high price tag had been something of a deterrent to purchase.

There was a sad ending to the Bond saga. In 1966, to bolster up their sagging three-wheeler business, they produced the very odd-looking '875', which had the Hillman Imp's engine, transaxle, and rear suspension under the skin. It did not sell at all well and soon the company was not making the profits it had been hoping for.

Closure, or a merger, was inevitable, but it was a real shock to see the announcement, in January 1969, that Reliant (of Tamworth) were to take over Bond. Tom Gratrix left Bond, to a new post in the motor trade, while Reliant (with 2000 workers) decided what they could do with Bond (just 300 workers).

The answer was, not a lot. No attempt was made to improve, or freshen-up, the existing cars, and although a so-called new Bond (the

ABOVE *Yes, OK, the Dutton is very much a purpose-built (kit-built) chassis, but it still uses elements of the Herald/Vitesse front suspension and steering as well*

TOP *Hiding a Herald-type chassis and mechanical components is this Marlin, with fibreglass body and something akin to an Alfa Romeo style of the 1930s*

CENTRE *Would you believe that under this style are the elements of a Herald/Vitesse layout, but a 2.5-litre engine, even larger and more powerful than that of a Vitesse 2-litre?*

Reliant-engined 'Bug') was launched in the summer of 1970, this was always built at Tamworth. The last Bond four-wheelers were produced in August 1970.

The 'specials'

Since the Herald and Vitesse models went out of production, quite a few specials have been put on sale using their chassis as a basis. In general, this involves the strip down and rebuilding of old Triumph models, discarding their rusty (and perhaps incomplete) body-shells, and fitting a smart new fibreglass shell instead. In some cases these new styles are modern, and in others they are unashamedly traditional. Nowadays, it is not wise to look at a so-called MG TF in the middle-distance, and believe first impressions; a closer scrutiny might reveal the familiar Herald or Vitesse front suspension, and Triumph engines, under a glossy shell.

Developments in the kit-car field are rapid, and the turnover of companies regular, so there is no point in quoting a definitive list of the 'specials' which have used Triumph components. However, I am much indebted to Roger Powell, who is the 'specials registrar' of the Triumph Sports Six Club (see the next chapter), for helping me merely to mention these makes:

Burlington is a marque based at Leamington Spa, not far away from the old Triumph factory at Coventry. The Burlington SS is a 1950s style sports car, with a great visual similarity to the current Morgan, which uses Herald chassis and running gear. The body-shell, in fact, is partly fibreglass, and partly aluminium, on a wooden frame.

Another Burlington model is the Chieftain, which is really a Second World War Jeep lookalike, also with Herald running gear, while the Burlington Arrow is another sports car, this time 1930s style, with cycle-type wings, though this is a real home mechanic machine, as sets of plans are sold which allow the customer to make his own modifications, but it is intended to use Herald components.

The **Gentry** is a well-known pseudo MG TF car, with a style almost identical to that famous traditional-looking Abingdon model. I have even seen Triumph chassis'd and engined Gentry cars carrying MG badges which, together with the use of a fibreglass bodyshell, must be enough to give any MG enthusiast a heart attack!

Then there was the **Marlin**, originally seen in 1979, which had an Alfa Romeo 1930s style body in mixed aluminium and fibreglass atop Herald/Vitesse mechanical components, and in which the engine was set back several inches from the standard Triumph position. More than 100 of these kit-cars were built by mid-1981, at which point the company introduced its own stiffer chassis design, intended to take Morris (BL) mechanical parts. Marlins were built at Plymouth, in Devon.

The **Moss** marque, of Sheffield, South Yorkshire, has already introduced three different Triumph-based models, in a five-year period. The oldest-looking is the Roadster, which (like the Burlington SS) looks similar to a Morgan of the period, or perhaps the MG TF, and can be sold as a complete car, or as a kit of parts. The example pictured on these pages has a Daimler V8-250 saloon radiator grille (without the Daimler badge!) on its sloping-back nose.

The Malvern is a stretched version of the Roadster, supposed to have 2+2 accommodation, and looks rather similar to the four-seater Morgan. Finally there is the Moss Mamba, also using all the chassis and mechanical parts of a Herald, but with a 1960s style, with full-width wings, which some people liken to an Alfa Romeo of the period.

The **Royale** is another 'replicar', actually with a style rather similar to that of the Burlington SS (similar in looks, in other words, to a Morgan), available as a complete car, or as a kit.

Finally, in this short survey, there was the **Spartan**, a kit which is no longer available from the Nottinghamshire-based manufacturer. The Spartan Car Co., was set up by Jim McIntyre in 1973, and made an MG TF-inspired two-seater kit, in which the traditional lines were perhaps spoilt by a rather upright front grille, and a somewhat ungainly hood and passenger compartment. Like the other cars mentioned here, it originally used a Herald or Vitesse chassis, but from the mid-1970s a purpose-built chassis frame, suitable for rigid rear axle use, was provided, and the use of Herald components fell away.

Amphicar: the best 'Triumph Special'

I could not resist mentioning the Amphicar, even though its only connection with the Triumph Herald was the 1147 cc engine, rated at 38 bhp. It was what its name implies—a vehicle which could be used as a road car, or as an amphibious vehicle. Need I also say, in truth, that it was not particularly good at either job?

The Amphicar was Hans Trippel's invention, and evolved from a 1959 prototype (titled the Eurocar Alligator) which had a BMC/Austin A35 engine. The definitive Amphicar of 1961, was still a strange-looking device, a high-off-the-ground convertible, with the Herald engine behind the driving compartment. Drive, on land, was by conventional means, but on the water it was by twin propellers. On land, it could struggle up to more than 60 mph, but on water six knots (or seven mph in landlubber's language) was flat out.

On land, the Amphicar was a pretty awful machine, which suffered from considerable oversteer, and had floppy steering, though at least it was a reasonably neat open four-seater, with a big luggage compartment up front. To turn it into a boat, one simply drove down a suitable slipway, engaged the appropriate propeller drive, made sure that the extra door seals were in operation, and forged ahead, using the front wheels to steer (very approximately) a plodding course!

Trippel never expected his Amphicars, which were built in Berlin, West Germany, to be sea-going craft, though one crossed the English channel in 1962 (and two more in 1965) to prove a point. The 1965 expedition was intended to prove how versatile the Amphicar was, for the trip was to the Frankfurt Motor Show—the eight-hour Channel crossing merely being a part of a long journey!

This Gentry carries an MG TF lookalike body style, an MG badge (and maybe even a BMC engine . . .) but the chassis and suspension is basically Triumph

Although *Autocar* actually borrowed an Amphicar while I was on their testing staff in the 1960s, I kept well clear of it (and, having talked to colleagues John Davey and Martin Lewis, I reckon I was wise . . .), as I was not keen to go for an involuntary swim, fully clothed, in the Thames on that occasion. *Autocar* didn't sink theirs, but I understand that other people did, and the Amphicar faded (sank?) gently from the scene in 1968.

Motor probably summed up the whole project perfectly in 1967, when their testers wrote that: '. . . it is not really a joke, of course, it's just that the wretched craft gets its identities all topsy-turvy by taking on the appearance of a sinking convertible in water, and a pop-eyed tadpole on land. Somehow, it looks a bit alien to its surroundings whatever they are. For this reason, we wouldn't go along with the brochure which claims that it is "the driving qualities of a modern, sporty type car. . . ."'

Thank goodness that the reputation of the Herald engine, at least, never suffered from this reputation. The Standard-Triumph engineers, incidentally, had a look at the design before it went into production in 1961–62, to be sure that the installation would be properly cooled, and lubricated. I worked at Coventry at the time, and seem to remember that no-one really wanted to drive the Amphicar, unless it was essential. . . .

Chapter 12
Front-wheel-drive 1300s and Toledos

As I have already pointed out, Standard-Triumph and the Herald project were saved from imminent disaster by the Leyland Motors takeover. After an initial period, while the new directors from Leyland (including Sir Henry Spurrier) fought to stem the financial losses, there was an amazing burst of activity on the engineering front. Just one of the projects to be considered was a new small-medium saloon which might, at one time, have replaced the Herald.

Sir Henry had been dismayed, when taking up office, to discover that the new-model programme was in some disarray. While it was true that preparations to launch the TR4 sports car were well advanced, and that approval had already been given to tool-up for the 'Atom', or Vitesse, the 'Bomb' (Spitfire) and 'Sabrina' (TRS twin-cam engine) projects were in limbo, development work was forging ahead on a tractor ('Zero') with which to attack Massey-Ferguson, there was talk of producing dumper trucks, and the 'Zebu' project (a large-car Vanguard replacement) had recently been cancelled.

Spitfire, Vitesse, 12/50 and Triumph 2000 projects were all speedily commissioned—in fact it was a miracle that so many new models could be put on sale in such a short time—after which Harry Webster and his engineers began to think deeply about a new smaller car. For the first few months, there was more talking than designing, but by November 1961 it had been agreed, at director level, that a 'new Herald' was to be in production by March 1964, which meant that the external styling had to be settled by March 1962; provision was to be made for two-door or four-door versions.

At this stage, however, there were several important changes in philosophy from the technical layout of the Herald/Vitesse cars. The new car, already coded 'Ajax', was to have a conventional pressed-steel unit-construction bodyshell, no convertible or estate car derivatives were to be designed—and it was to have front-wheel-drive!

Harry Webster was at first determined to replace the Herald with a new front-wheel-drive saloon. In November 1962, the clay and wooden mock-up of the proposed car looked like this, with slightly hooded headlamps

It was Harry Webster himself who made all the original sketches for the mechanical layout of 'Ajax', and it was his close friend and associate, Giovanni Michelotti, who was to style the car. Curiously enough, there was very little doubt, at any stage, about Webster's choice of transmission, and front-wheel-drive

The 'new Herald', or 'Ajax' project, now seen on mock-up form in January 1963, still not equipped with the bulbous forehead which would follow for the production machine. The basic proportions, however, are already settling

January 1963 (at a time when the 12/50 was just ready to go on sale) finds the front-wheel-drive mock-up at this stage, looking as if it might be a two-door car. There was a long way to go, still

layout, but a great deal of controversy over the styling. Michelotti's problems not only included the brief to get costs down as much as decently possible, but the sheer practical problem of producing a graceful shape around the nose, where the engine-on-top-of-transmission layout chosen resulted in a rather tall block of cast iron.

The delays mounted—not only because of the styling problem, but because in that first year, 1962, when the initial work took place, the Herald suddenly began to boom, profits began to be made, and the urgency of a successor slipped further and further into the background. There were several full-blooded rows at director level (managing director Stanley Markland, ex-Leyland Motors, was a very robust character. . . .)

Styling approval of 'Ajax' was not given until May 1963, with a provisional launch pencilled in for Autumn 1965, and with £3.25 million allocated for capital investment. Significantly, Standard-Triumph car production had just risen to 3000 units a week, which was highly profitable for the corporation. Body/chassis units were to be tooled, and produced, at the expanding Standard-Triumph factory at Speke, near Liverpool.

Some years ago, Harry Webster told me all about the evolution of the mechanical layout, and extracts from this interview are quite enthralling:

'Effectively I was still my own product-planner in the early 1960s, and I had a good look round at what other people were doing, and which way the smaller motor cars appeared to be developing. Of course we—first Alick, then Stanley Markland and myself—were much influenced by what Issigonis was up to at Longbridge. The Mini had worked well right from the start, and then, while we were scheming the 'Ajax', he produced the 1100 Morris as well.'

HGW had been sketching front-wheel-drive layouts for more than ten years before he got down to the 'Ajax' design, in detail. In 1962–3, however, he thought it time to analyse the possibilities completely, and as he said to 'Steady' Barker in an *Autocar* feature:

'We didn't enter into it lightly, and in fact we did a complete brochure of various types of engine-transmission layouts including the across-the-chassis type. . . . If I had another chance (he was talking three years after the event) I would do something very similar, not identical, but still with the engine fore-and-aft. . . .'

On looks, and in regard to its market 'slot', the company's view of the new car had clearly changed in four years:

'Of course, before the 2000 was introduced we knew there was going to be a need for a car between it and the Herald . . . that was our guiding principle all along. In fact the Triumph 1300 body structure is very like that of the 2000, and so are a lot of other things such as the semi-trailing arm rear suspension, the boxed front wings and so on. . . . It has the same look and quality—it's a 2000 Junior.'

What factors influenced the choice of front-wheel-drive?

'If you consider the 1300, in proportion to its overall length we've probably got more fore-and-aft seating capacity than any other car we've made. . . . We wanted the longest possible wheelbase within an established overall length . . . roadholding is better, of course. . . . Incidentally, I wonder whether you've spotted that with the main shaft where it is, by putting a flange on the end of it one could easily make a very nice four-wheel-drive of it!'

Yet none of this should hide the fact that the Triumph 1300 of 1965, which *Autocar* described in their road test as standing alone 'as the best small car currently available', was no longer meant to be a replacement for the Herald. That requirement had gone by the board even while the car was at the mock-up, and design stages, when it became clear that a '2000 Junior' was more immediately needed, rather than a stripped down motor car to replace the famous separate-chassis model, whose reputation was still building up.

ABOVE *The anatomy of the 1296 cc engine, and the cleverly detailed Triumph 1300 front-wheel-drive transmission, laid bare*

CENTRE *The finalised front-wheel-drive Triumph 1300 package, showing the familiar engine, placed rather high. The rubber drive shaft 'doughnuts' later to find a home at the rear of the Vitesse 2-litre Mk 2 are just visible at the inner ends of the shafts, under the cross-member. This engine formed the basis of the 13/60 unit*

ABOVE *Well before launch, the 'new Herald' outgrew itself, and the 'Ajax' project eventually developed into a smart, costly, and altogether more up-market four-door saloon. Two years later, the 1300 TC, complete with twin-carbs and 75 bhp, arrived*

TOP *Later, when the car was launched as the Triumph 1300, technical director Harry Webster posed with models and sketches to show how it had all evolved. The model, by the way, looks very close to the November 1962 style*

It is interesting, indeed, to note that when the 1300 went on sale in January 1966, UK total prices were as follows:

Triumph Herald 1200 saloon	£592
Triumph Herald 12/50 saloon	£648
Triumph Vitesse 1600	£758
Triumph 1300	£797

The 1300, therefore, was more expensive even than the Vitesse 1600, and no less than 34 per cent more costly than the 1200 saloon.

By 1970, however, Triumph, now part of the unwieldy British Leyland Motor Corporation, had foreseen the imminent end of the Herald/Vitesse family, and had rejigged the 1300 design to take account of this. In a very complicated re-launch, the 1300 was up-engined, to become the 1500, still with front-wheel-drive, while a radically redesigned, and cheapened derivative, was the Toledo, in which the underpan was revamped, a rear-wheel-drive installation was fitted up, and independent rear suspension was abandoned in favour of a rigid rear axle.

If ever there was to have been a Herald replacement, the Toledo should have been it, but it lacked the character, and the style, of the older car, and the public were not impressed. Prices? Well, at the Earls Court Motor Show of 1970, where the Herald was seen for the last time, and the Toledo was seen for the first, this was the comparison:

Herald 13/60 saloon	£848
Toledo (2-door)	£889
1500 (4-door, front-wheel-drive)	£1113
Vitesse 2-litre saloon	£1082

That was not the end of the story, of course, but nothing which followed had any relevance to the Heralds and Vitesses. A four-door Toledo followed, the 1500 became 'TC' with rear-wheel-drive in 1973, and that layout also spawned the single-cam Dolomite and 16-valve Dolomite Sprint models into the bargain. The last of these was built in 1980, and with their death the faithful old four-cylinder engine, first seen in 1953, died as well.

As for four-wheel-drive, it never happened in a passenger car, but the conversion *was* applied to a chunky lightweight commercial vehicle, called 'Pony', designed in Coventry, but actually built from 1966 by Autocars in Israel.

This was what 'the new Herald' might have been in the mid-1960s, if the marketing thrust had not altered. In mid-1970, Triumph finally launched the Toledo, which was a much different development of the original 'Ajax'/1300 style, for this car had rear-wheel-drive, a two-door saloon body, and a 1296 cc engine, allied to simple furnishings in the Herald 13/60 style

This was one of the very first prototype slant-four engines to run, complete with overhead camshaft valve gear, and was of the type eventually sold in big numbers to Saab in Sweden, and in the Triumph Dolomites of the 1970s. I recall that, at one time, the Dolomite might have been called 'Vitesse'

Appendix 1 Triumph Sports Six Club: keeping the cars alive

By 1970, production of Heralds and Vitesses was almost on 'automatic pilot', with no new development taking place, with new models like the Toledos and Dolomites, coming on, and with little interest being shown in the cars by management, motoring press, and most overseas markets. It would be wrong to say that the Herald died a lonely death, but it was certainly mourned only by a few enthusiasts.

In the next few years, the Spitfire remained in full-scale, and very successful, production, to keep the 'separate chassis' reputation alive, but the memory of the family cars slipped further and further into the background. In an earlier era, that would have been that. Very few well-kept examples would have survived, and these would have had no more than curiosity value.

But not in the 1970s. The 'classic car' movement burgeoned, more and more interest began to be shown in cars of character built *after*, rather than *before*, the Second World War. Character? Heralds and Vitesses certainly had plenty of that, but they were increasingly coming to be neglected by the factory. So, what to do?

John Griffiths, president of the one-make club which grew up around these cars, now takes up the story:

'It started in July 1977, when a man called Paul Swanson put an advert in *Exchange and Mart*, and in *Thoroughbred & Classic Cars*. There were 13 initial replies, of which I was one. We had a meeting, at a motorway service station, and we got things started from there. We gave people individual jobs, and started recruiting more members.

'At that moment there was no club specifically for the cars we wanted to preserve. There had been, at one stage, a Vitesse Owners' Club in Coventry, but that was very small, and eventually fizzled out. Other than that, there was Club Triumph of course, but that encompassed all Triumph cars, and other Triumph clubs, and wasn't as specific either.'

So, there was no one-make club for the cars covered in this book, neither was there even an embryo 'Herald restoration' industry, of small concerns which have done so much, in recent years, to provide parts and service back-up for these cars.

'In 1977, we all had to rely on our dealers, and on British Leyland,' John Griffiths says, 'for spares, but there were no specialists.'

The club, of course, needed a distinctive name, and this caused a great deal of heart searching among the officers.

'Somebody wanted to call it VODKA—which was Vitesse Owners, Drivers . . . and something, but we decided against that. We wanted to encompass all the six cars to be eligible—Herald, Vitesse, Spitfire, GT6, the Bonds, and Specials. There were six types of car, which explains the 'Six' in the name. In addition to that, 'Sports Six' was the name given to the Vitesse when it was exported to the United States, so it seemed to be appropriate to call ourselves the Triumph Sports Six Club.

'A few people seem to think it's only for six-cylinder cars, but now we've changed the club logo to show all the cars spread out under the Triumph badge, there doesn't seem to be any confusion.'

Every club, of course, needs aims and ambitions, to be viable, and in the case of the new TSSC, these were simple: To promote and preserve the Herald chassis'd vehicles. There was, after all, no sign of this being done anywhere else, particularly by British Leyland itself. There was no doubt that, given the means, such a club could provide a much-needed service for frustrated Triumph owners.

The Newport Pagnell meeting, held on the last day of July in 1977, was very significant, for this was what the club policy agreed:

'To build up a stock of spare parts, on behalf of members, and to endeavour to keep a central store. To encourage pride of ownership in these classic cars, to attain national recognition for the club, and its aims, to find the oldest member car in the club, to establish some form of library whereby technical data, parts manuals, and workshop manuals could either be borrowed or

TSSC's Leicester Area 'Bonanza' in August 1984 had this massive gathering of Herald-family cars. The Herald's appeal lives on!

photocopied, and thereby lent to members, to establish a scheme whereby specialist tools for specific work could be loaned or borrowed. To organize rallies, social functions, etc, and to have a regular newsletter.'

Following an approach to British Leyland, approval was granted to use the Triumph badge in the club's logo, and paperwork, and some links were forged with the company through the public relations network, but this has never been an important feature, and appears to have lapsed, somewhat, in recent years.

The TSSC's original president was Paul Swanson, with John Griffiths as vice-president, but once the club had reached a membership of one thousand, Paul withdrew completely from the scene, and John Griffiths took over. Both these personalities had Vitesses, when the club was formed, John's convertible now being progressively modified, and used in sprints and hillclimbs.

When the club was started, no-one had any idea of the size that it would reach in such a short time. The club now (1985) proudly boasts that it is: 'The World's Largest Triumph Club', but in the early days it was thought that only cars like the Vitesse and perhaps the GT6 would become fashionable 'collectors' cars.

John Griffiths, indeed, subscribed to that theory at first, and had the Vitesse convertible to back his conviction. Then, for the 1980 Round Britain Tour, organized by the club to celebrate the Herald's 21st birthday, he borrowed a Herald 12/50 to use, came back quite converted to four-cylinder motoring as well, and now has two Heralds *and* the Vitesse in this stable!

The growth rate, indeed, was quite slow at first, and the projected 'maximum' membership of 1000 was not achieved until 1980. Then things began to 'take off', extra growth has been phenomenal, and by the time the first edition of this book is published there should be more than 6000 members.

What caused this explosion? Probably the 'chain reaction' syndrome helped, but the existence of a very good monthly publication, *The Courier*, which got even better in the early 1980s when it began to be edited by the club's first paid consultant, Bill Sunderland, must have helped a lot. The bigger the club became, the more publicity it gained, and the more new members joined up. From a start, in July 1977, with 13 founder members, the thousand mark was reached in August 1980, and the 5000 barrier was breached in August 1984.

Is there a limit? Presumably there is, but a look at the breakdown of cars on the register, and comparison with total build figures suggested that there is a long way to go.

In the spring of 1985, and in round figures, cars on the register were:

Heralds	1500
Vitesses	2000
Spitfires	2000
GT6s	1200
Bonds	150
Specials	100
Total	6950

On average, during the winter of 1984–85, up to 250 new members were joining every month, and with the club's very resourceful new car insurance scheme coming on stream, a further doubling of membership looked likely for the near future.

Such a growing club needed to split itself down into local areas, and this has now successfully been done. At the time of writing, there are more than 50 areas, who hold local meetings, in the UK alone. The overseas aspect is still in its infancy (John Griffiths: 'That is an element that is still untapped, as far as we are concerned. We have had an overseas affiliation secretary for a number of years, and we have contact with a number of overseas clubs, from South Africa, right throughout Europe, of course, Australia, New Zealand, the United States—but there isn't a TSSC of the USA, or anything like that'), but this is a future development, I'm sure.

When the club was founded, parts supply for the Herald and Vitesse was still assured, even several years after production had ceased, though parts prices were rising fast, and supply depended very much on the attitude of the local Triumph dealer—it helped enormously if he had been involved with the cars, right from the end of the 1950s.

Following club recognition by British Leyland, discounts became available from authorized dealers, but a more important development was that specialized concerns were founded, and grew up, to service, repair, and restore cars in this family. That was, and will always be, a very important feature in the preservation of any car, long out of production. Because one of the club members' main enthusiasms is for concours contests, where the cars have to look their best. The search for correct parts, or correctly re-manufactured parts, goes on all the time.

The parts merchandising side of BL, Unipart, still stocks many items for the cars covered in this book, but some items, when out of stock, are no longer re-ordered. This is reasonable, perhaps, when one remembers that even the youngest Herald is 15 years old (in 1985). Major items like chassis frames have not been available, from Unipart, for some time, although parts of that frame such as outriggers are still available, though some private-enterprise frames have already been produced, and will presumably become more significant in the years to come.

Major body panels, such as door skins, wings and some bonnet pressings are still available from Unipart, as are supplies of glass (windscreen, side and back light) for most of the derivatives. Mechanically, in fact, there is no failure which should keep a Herald or Vitesse permanently off the road, though it may be a matter of time, and certainly money, before major items in the drive line can be rebuilt, and restored to health. But, in regard to suspension and steering components, and other 'consumables' in the braking system, there should be no hang-up for some years.

The most important TSSC innovation in the recent past has been to set up a special insurance scheme for club members' cars. John Griffiths told me that:

'It was becoming increasingly difficult for club members to obtain competitive insurance quotations, and secondly it was very difficult to obtain "Agreed Value" insurance. Now, as these cars became more and more valuable, members—especially those restoring cars—wanted to protect their interests. We wanted to arrange a no-nonsense agreed value insurance scheme, and as we were going to administer it as well, we also wanted to make it a fully comprehensive scheme. It's had a great reception already.'

So, after this, where is the Club going next? Response from the officers, quite literally, was—bigger, rapidly! They see no sign of the membership level topping out for some time to come, and to service this obvious demand they intend to go even more strongly into the location, stocking, and provisioning of spares for the cars.

There is also the 'Self-Help' scheme, which may be unique in what it offers. Members, in effect, are invited to make themselves available as TSSC 'breakdown men', so that if another member had a mishap in their area, he could make a local telephone call, ask for help—a town, the loan of jacks, spare wheels, tools or whatever, maybe even an emergency night's lodging—and hope to receive help very shortly. As another car firm's advertising says: Simple, but Efficient.

With a club like this, expanding all the time, the Herald and Vitesse family's future is surely secure.

Appendix 2 **Spitfire and GT6: the sports car derivatives**

Even in 1957, when the entire Zobo concept was still very fluid, Alick Dick, Martin Tustin and Harry Webster were already thinking of designing a whole series of cars on the same chassis. One of those derivatives, no more than a vaguely considered pipe-dream at that stage, was a sports car. It took another five years, until October 1962, before the very first Spitfire was revealed.

By August 1957, when the Zobo project suddenly picked up momentum, the sports car style got its first official mention in company records, but thereafter it disappeared into limbo. Only in the spring of 1960, a full year after the Herald had been launched, was it seriously considered once again. At that time, no decisions had been made on a style, or even on bodyshell construction (fibreglass construction was certainly discussed at this stage), but with the TR3A selling very well, everyone agreed that it was the right thing to do.

In the meantime, a lot had happened. Commercially, Standard-Triumph had gone through a real upheaval, as I have already described. Alick Dick was busily trying to secure body suppliers for the future, and expanding Canley's capacity at the same time. A big new assembly hall was well on the way to completion. The Herald was already in trouble in the showrooms, and the UK market was about to take a nosedive as a government credit squeeze was applied.

Out in the market place, the nascent small-sports-car market had already been electrified by the arrival of the new Austin-Healey Sprite which, though thought ugly by many people, was a chirpy and nimble little two-seater already selling in large numbers. By the spring and summer of 1960, it was already known, through motor industry gossip, that the Sprite was being re-styled, and that there would be an MG-badged version of it as well.

John Carpenter, looking back on his years at Standard-Triumph, recalls that:

'. . . the idea of building a small sports car started with Harry Webster. I'm sure we all developed the feeling that the TR now needed a smaller vehicle alongside it. It seemed to some of us that there was a niche for a smaller, inexpensive little car at a price above the Sprite but below the level of MGA and TR, and of course it was the American market that we were going to rely on. America was the platform on which all sports car volume was based.'

I have already written a complete book about the birth, development, and career, of the Herald-derived sports cars (*Triumph Spitfire and GT6*, Osprey Publishing, 1982), which is actually the companion volume to this book, but the story of the Herald and Vitesse would be incomplete without a summary of the Spitfire.

The important point to remember is that although the Spitfire arrived more than three years after the launch of the Herald, it was in continuous production until the autumn of 1980—in fact being the very last of the separate-chassis Triumphs to be made, In a career spanning 18 years, there were 314,342 Spitfires built, along with 40,926 examples of the six-cylinder GT6 models.

The whole idea of the Spitfire—or 'Bomb' as it was code-named at the time—evolved in a series of discussions between Harry Webster and Giovanni Michelotti. During 1959 and 1960, when Harry was making frequent trips to Turin to Michelotti's studios, the concept of a short-wheelbase two-seater began to emerge. It was soon decided that the sports car should have a wheelbase of 83 inches (8.5 inches shorter than the Herald itself, but three inches longer than that of the Sprite, which was already identified as the principal rival), and that as much existing Herald hardware as possible should be employed.

To get things started, a complete 948 cc Herald was driven out to Turin, where Michelotti's craftsmen dismantled the body, carved the chassis about, and started building a prototype. The Italian had already submitted several sketches, Tustin, Turnbull and Webster had chosen a style, and work began on a wooden buck.

The Spitfire sports car chassis, though unique, had obvious family connections to that of the Herald, as this study of a 1965 Mk 2 model makes clear

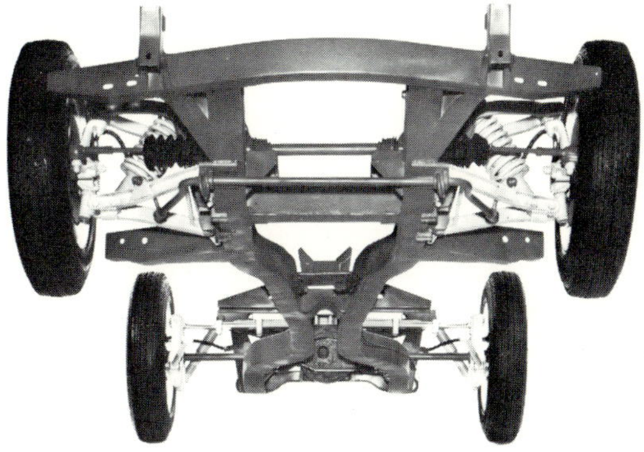

This was the underside view of the Mk 3 Spitfire's rolling chassis, showing the way that Herald front suspension, steering and rear suspension components were all used

To set the record straight, I should say that the shortened Herald chassis only ever figured at the mock-up and original prototype Bomb, for right from the start it was the intention to give the sports car a purpose-built chassis frame. Although this still picked up the Herald-style independent front suspension, swing axle rear suspension, rack-and-pinion steering, and all the same basic engine, transmission and final drive equipment, it was of different layout, with more solid 'backbone' members cradling the drive line, with stiffer, more stubby, outriggers, but with no longitudinal side-members. The rear suspension damper 'bridge' was of Vitesse/'Star' frame type, rather than that of the original Herald.

It was possible to produce a frame of this configuration because Webster and Arthur Ballard had now been able to consider using a bodyshell with one-piece welded up floor and underside, into which strong box-section sills, under the doors, could be incorporated. By the time detail body design began in 1960, the Mulliners/Forward Radiator business had been completely absorbed into Standard-Triumph, and it was decided that complete body manufacture should be carried out at Forward Radiator. Unlike the Herald, the bodyshell would be completely welded together, with the exception of the combined bonnet and front wings, which were pivoted in the extreme nose in the same way as the Herald. The same type of bonnet latching, ahead of the doors on each side of the car, was used.

(At the same time as the Bomb was being developed, a short wheelbase Herald was built in Coventry. This car, which carried chassis number X661, compared with X659 for the first Bomb, used convertible body panels, all the shortening of the wheelbase being accommodated in the area of the doors. It was painted in battleship grey, had a rather sketchy hood and sidescreens, and looked thoroughly disreputable and unloved by the time I first saw it in 1961. It was only useful as a Bomb development 'mule', but had become a much-abused hack within a year. I should point out, though, that it had the best handling of any Herald I ever drove.)

Construction of the original prototype, which used all the instruments and switchgear of the Herald which had gone to Turin earlier that year, started during the summer of 1960, and after belated approval of the project by management, it was delivered to Coventry before the end of October 1960. Almost immediately, however, it was stowed away under a dust sheet, undeveloped and little used, for the company was rapidly running out of funds for investment.

Then, in the autumn of 1961, as is now well known, Leyland's Stanley Markland was given a guided tour of the experimental department by Harry Webster, spotted an unfamiliar shape under a sheet, demanded to see it, and almost immediately authorized its development, and tooling. Press tools, some of rather a temporary nature at first, were produced by Mulliners/Forward radiator, chassis tooling was produced by Sankeys, and the mechanical specification was quickly settled.

Except for different rates and settings for springs and dampers, the complete suspension installation was as Herald, as was the rack-and-pinion steering gear and the 16 inch diameter steering wheel. The gearbox and final drive, including their components and ratios, were all the same, but the 1147 cc engine was made considerably more powerful. For 1963, the Herald 1200 engine produced 39 bhp (net) at 4500 rpm, whereas the Spitfire's peak power was boosted to 63 bhp (net) at 5750 rpm. This 62 per cent improvement was produced by the use of a high compression ratio, twin HS2 ($1\frac{1}{4}$ in. choke) SU carburettors, and a more sporting camshaft grind, complete with higher lift. The cylinder head casting, however, was still that of the 1200.

In the next few years, much more development effort was directed to the sports car than to the Herald range. Named 'Spitfire', reputably following a brainwave from the company's new sales director, Donald Stokes, it soon became a sales success all over the world (and particularly in North America), and it was regularly up-dated to keep ahead of the MG Midget/Austin-Healey Sprite models. Statisticians will be delighted to know that the Spitfire persistently outsold the opposition from BMC, even though there were 'badge-engineered' versions to confuse the issue.

A year after launch, the Spitfire was made available with a detachable hardtop, Laycock overdrive, and centre lock wire-spoke wheels, none of which ever featured on the Herald itself (though enthusiasts have added them to their own cars in later years), and from the spring of 1965 it was up-dated to become Spitfire Mk 2. This version featured a bit more power (67 bhp) by which time the 12/50 saloon was on sale with 51 bhp, still from a single carburettor, and slightly more luxurious trim and furnishings.

The Spitfire Mk 3, announced in March 1967, was a much improved machine, not only faster, but more stylish than before. Although it still used the same basic chassis, running gear, and body pressings, it had been freshened up by the fitment of a raised 'bone-in-the-teeth' front bumper, and there was a new and altogether more sophisticated foldaway soft top mechanism.

The engine came in for a lot of attention. Not only was it enlarged to 1296 cc (several months ahead of its adoption for the Herald 13/60, but well over a year behind the front-wheel-drive 1300 model), but it was also given the new type of eight port cylinder head. This had also been introduced for the 1300, and would also figure in the Herald 13/60.

Thus equipped, the Mk 3 had 75 bhp, and had the beating of its opposition for some years to come. However, with activity on the Herald running down, but with North American sales holding up remarkably well, more investment was poured into the sports cars. The Mk IV (not Mk 4, for some marketing quirk . . .) was launched in November 1970, and although it looked superficially the same as the familiar Mk 3, it actually had completely new front and rear body skins. At the front there were concealed welded seams on the bonnet for the first time, and different location of panel joints, while at the rear there was a more integrated style incorporating a flatter boot lid, a chopped-off tail like those of the Stag and the TR6, a full width rear bumper, more elegant tail lamps and (still as an option) a more angular hardtop with extra glass and a near-flat rear window).

The engine had slightly less power than before (redefined to DIN measurement, it produced 63 bhp at 6000 rpm)—this being because of the onset of more severe emission laws in North America, but to counteract this there was an all-synchromesh gearbox, which had evolved from that of the Vitesse 2-litre, and a new type of swing-spring rear suspension.

'Swing-spring' installations were nothing new to Standard-Triumph, for John Lloyd specifically remembers a prototype being built at Banner Lane in 1958 or 1959, even before the Herald was put on the market. Visually, there was little difference between 'swing-spring' and

At the London Motor Show of 1963, Triumph showed this magnificently prepared Spitfire rolling chassis, and any Herald owner will be able to see the many components also shared with this model

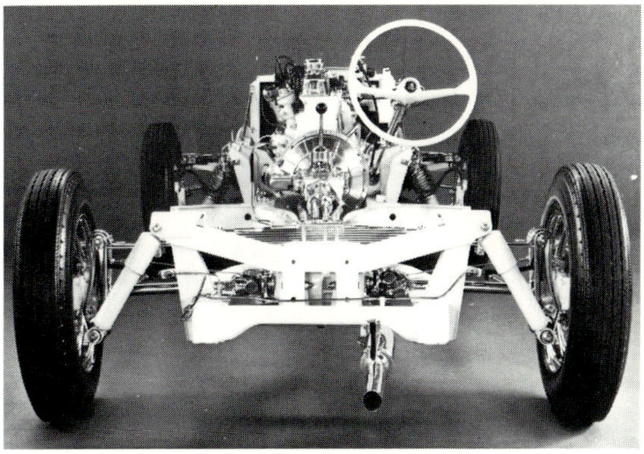

The Spitfire chassis from behind, showing the chassis 'bridge' which is almost identical to that used in the Vitesse, and Herald 'Star' frames as well

the more familiar type of swing-axle suspension, for fixed length half-shafts, angled telescopic dampers, and radius arms forward to the bodyshell (there were no rear outriggers on the Spitfire frame) were all retained.

The big difference was that with 'swing-spring' the transverse leaf spring actually pivoted on the top of the final drive casing, instead of being firmly bolted down to it. This meant that there was very little resistance to roll, and much reduced camber change at the rear wheels, though in one-wheel, or two-wheel bump conditions the suspension was as firm as usual.

With suitable attention to front suspension settings (the front anti-roll bar needed to be much stiffer, to restore the overall balance of the car), this cured the Herald/Spitfire tuck-under problem at a stroke, and the car handled much better than before. In their test report, *Autocar* said that this 'transforms the Spitfire's handling. . . . One of the most impressive things about the latest Spitfire is to be able to hurl it into a corner, lift off . . . and find the car still pointing where the driver aimed it. It seems almost impossible now to get the back wheels to tuck under and flick the car into a potentially frightening oversteer situation.'

How many fast-driving Herald owners would have loved that suspension on their cars!

Before it was upgraded again, the Mk IV was given a 1493 cc engine (Triumph 1500/1500TC size) to counteract the stifling effects of USA emission laws, then for 1975 it became the '1500' model, complete with 71 bhp (DIN) in Europe, and a genuine 100 mph maximum speed. Mk IV, incidentally, had featured a 3.89:1 final drive ratio, as found in the Vitesse 2-litre, whereas the 1500 had a ratio of 3.63:1, which was never found in any of the saloons. The 1500 carried on, virtually unchanged apart from cosmetic improvements, until August 1980, when the last car of all was built at the Canley assembly hall. From that point, Standard-Triumph at Coventry ceased to be an assembly plant, for the Dolomite saloons were withdrawn shortly afterwards.

The other sports car to evolve from the basic Herald/Vitesse design, of course, was the GT6, and I can easily summarize the blood-line by saying that GT6 was to Spitfire as Vitesse was to Herald—in other words a six-cylinder engine was neatly squeezed into the existing chassis frame, and chassis fittings upgraded to suit.

The style of the GT6, however, was first produced, in prototype form, on a four-cylinder Spitfire chassis, and the shape was first seen in public on the Le Mans and Tour de France competition Spitfires of 1964. The production car itself, however, was not put on sale until the autumn of 1966, with sales beginning more than four years after the original Vitesse, and more than seven years after the first of the Heralds.

I have already described, in chapter 5, how the 'Atom' project came into existence, and how this evolved into the Vitesse. The GT6 project, however, was not a direct result of this. As John Lloyd told me:

'What really happened was that having done the Spitfire, Harry (Webster) decided, with George Turnbull, to do a fast-back mini-E-Type, and Leslie Moore, our stylist, did one at the factory. It looked bloody awful . . . the roof was deep and bulbous. That's when Harry called in Michelotti again, and we shipped out a Spitfire, to make a four-cylinder "GT". . . .'

The prototype which returned to Coventry in the autumn of 1963 was a very pleasing car, absolutely right as far as the style was concerned, but too heavy for its 63 bhp Spitfire engine. Not only was it much less lively than the sports car, but it would have had to sell for a much higher price, and the sales department was not at all impressed.

Within months, therefore, the car was re-engined with a 1.6-litre six-cylinder Vitesse engine, having the latest type of Zenith-Stromberg carburettors (89 bhp at first, but only 77 bhp once various noise-reducing refinements had been added to it), and it was in that guise that the author took it to and from the Le Mans circuit before the race.

Later, and before the specification of the fastback car was finalized, it was decided to fit the larger engine both to the Vitesse and to this style, so the production car became a 95 bhp/1998 cc powered machine, and it took on the name of GT6. Mechanically it was almost identical to the Vitesse 2-litre in every way, while the body lines, apart from the fastback, were pure Spitfire Mk 2. The overall effect was made most pleasing by the addition of a new wood-trimmed facia/instrument board, while the top included a hatchback. Options included overdrive, and centre-lock wire wheels. It looked, and even sounded, rather like the mini-E-Type Webster had conceived three years earlier.

Unfortunately the GT6 handled in much the same way as the first of the Vitesse 2-litres, and since its direct rival was the very stable and elegant MG MGB GT, this attracted criticism. The result was that within two years a Mark 2 version was developed, and put on sale at the same time as the Vitesse 2-litre Mk 2 made its bow.

Not only did the GT6 Mk 2 have the same lower-wishbone rear suspension and the 104 bhp (net) of the Vitesse, but it was also given the 'bone-in-teeth' front bumper, a tasteful new facia design, and cabin air outlets in the rear quarters. Not only that, but the 3.27:1 final drive, previously only available on non-overdrive cars, became available with overdrive as well, which offered a really high-geared motorway cruiser; in due course, however, the sales department asked for the 3.89:1 overdrive ratio to be restored, and this was done.

There *was* a difference between saloon and sports coupé rear suspensions, however. Whereas the Vitesse Mk 2 had lever-arm dampers controlling the suspension, the GT6 Mk 2 had long telescopic dampers, whose top mounting was actually in the bodyshell, not on the chassis cross member.

There was one more GT6 derivative to come, and this was the Mk 3, introduced before the end of 1970, running through to the end of 1973 when the model was dropped. This car had the same re-skinned body style as the Spitfire Mk IV, including the cropped-off tail panels, though there were no significant mechanical changes. The lower-wishbone type of rear suspension was retained until the end of 1972, but for the car's last year it was given the swing-spring rear suspension of the Spitfire. Although theoretically inferior, the swing-spring system was perfectly adequate for its purpose, and it saw the GT6 out.

The GT6 was dropped several years before the Spitfire, mainly because sales were always rather more restricted (there were only 4218 swing-spring cars, of a total of 13,042 Mk 3s, for instance), and because it was becoming increasingly more costly to change the specification every year to keep the car 'road legal' in North America.

In their best combined year in North America—1972—no fewer than 9687 Spitfires and 2753 GT6s, 12,440 in all, were delivered, which made this a very successful and profitable

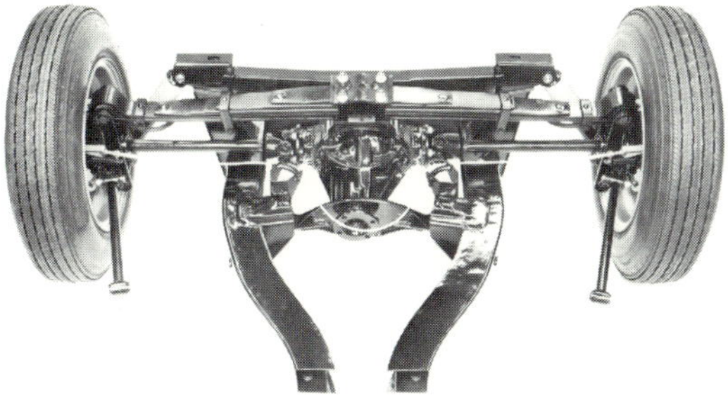

operation. The overall total sales achieved by each type of Spitfire and GT6 show just how well the Herald's basic architecture had been adapted. Here they are:

Spitfire Mk 1	45,573
Spitfire Mk 2	37,409
Spitfire Mk 3	65,320
Spitfire Mk IV	70,021
Spitfire 1500	95,829
Total:	314,342
GT6 Mk 1	15,818
GT6 Mk 2	12,066
GT6 Mk 3	13,042
Total:	40,926

ABOVE *If the Spitfire was the sporting version of the Herald, the GT6 was the sporting version of the Vitesse. This was the Mk 3 version, introduced in October 1970. Like the Vitesse Mk 2, it had a 104 bhp 1998 cc six-cylinder engine, and the lower-wishbone type of rear suspension, plus this sleek fastback coupé body style*

TOP LEFT *A neat and simple 'swing-spring' rear suspension was developed for the Mk IV Spitfire, for the 1970s, which cut out the camber change and oversteer problem for good, but this was never applied to the Herald itself. To the addicted modifier, of course, the change would be easy enough, for the only real difference is to the method of locating the spring on top of the differential casing*

TOP RIGHT *The original Spitfire sports car of 1962, with a shorter wheelbase than the Herald, and a 63 bhp engine tune, but still using many components common to the Herald 1200 itself*

LEFT ABOVE *For two years, Triumph campaigned fierce little 'works' racing Spitfires, with light alloy bodies, and with about 100 bhp from their 1147 cc engines. Here are three of the original four cars, at Le Mans in 1964*

Appendix 3 **Assembly in Coventry. 1959–71: all the facts and figures**

Over the years, I have assembled any number of statistics about Triumph car production, post-war. As is only to be expected in these matters, the figures offered sometimes conflict slightly, one with another.

What follows, therefore, is in certain cases a 'best guess' from information provided. The problem, of course, was that ownership of the Triumph marque changed several times during the 1960s and 1970s. Some management teams cherished their heritage, and the records which went with it, while others ordered a complete clear out. However, except for the fine detail of Herald assembly in 1959, 1960 and 1961, most necessary information has been preserved for posterity.

Here are the details of Coventry assembly during the relevant period covered by this book. Note that Completely Knocked Down (CKD) totals have not been separated by statisticians, except for the Herald 13/60 model.

Total production, by model and body type

			Total
Herald (948 cc)	saloon (incl. S)	76,860	
	Coupé	15,153	
	Convertible	8262	100,275
Herald 1200 (1147 cc)	saloon	201,142	
	Coupé	5319	
	Convertible	43,295	
	Estate	39,819	289,575
Herald 12/50 (1147 cc)	saloon	53,267	53,267
Herald 13/60 (1296 cc)	saloon	38,886	
	'Sunroof' saloon	1547	
	Convertible	11,772	
	Estate	15,467	
	(+CKD, not defined)	14,978	82,650
Vitesse 1600 (1596 cc)	saloon	22,814	
	Convertible	8447	31,261
Vitesse 2-litre (1998 cc) (Mks 1 and 2)	saloon	12,977	
	Convertible	6974	19,951
		Grand Total	*576,979*

In addition, an unknown number of Herald Courier vans were produced between 1962 and 1964.

The Spitfire and GT6 sports cars were of the same basic types, though with different (backbone-type) chassis frames. Total production of each was 314,342 (Spitfire) and 40,926 (GT6) respectively.

All in all, cars of the Herald family (but excluding the sports cars) were in production for 150 consecutive months, at an average rate of about 3750 cars/month.

This figure, however, was beaten by the achievements of the SC range of cars (Standard 8, 10, and Pennant), built between 1953–59, which were produced at an average rate of 4750 cars a month. Their overall total was 351,727.

Running rings round the opposition? Many Herald enthusiasts think these cars always have done just that!

The earlier Triumph Mayflower, built for only three years in the early 1950s, was built at the rate of 920 cars/month. The overall total was 35,000.

Standard-Triumph factories' production, by company financial year (October to September), from mid-1950s to early 1970s

The following table is an amalgam of two distinct documents, made available at various times, during the 1970s. Following the wholesale rebuilding of the Coventry site, no further detail is now available, but the trends exhibited are interesting:

Financial Year	*Total Standard-Triumph production*	*Coventry production (built-up)*	*Liverpool production (built-up)*	*CKD*
1956–57	48,835	n.a.	n.a.	—
1957–58	76,539	n.a.	—	n.a.
1958–59	85,926	n.a.	—	n.a.
1959–60	138,762	n.a.	—	n.a.
1960–61	78,735	n.a.	—	n.a.
1961–62	78,383	66,807	—	11,576
1962–63	100,764	86,553	—	14,211
1963–64	119,937	107,284	—	12,653
1964–65	121,405	105,528	—	15,877
1965–66	118,398	103,851	—	14,547
1966–67	117,350	98,016	—	19,334
1967–68	139,488	117,927	—	21,561
1968–69	132,322	102,595	—	29,727
1969–70	112,127	90,799	776	20,552
1970–71	134,350	95,711	20,576	18,063
1971–72	138,666	100,804	26,549	11,313

NOTE: The Liverpool factory started assembling Triumph Toledos in the summer of 1970. The last Herald/Vitesse product—a Herald 13/60 Estate—was built in May 1971.

Index